THE SIGN
of the
SON OF MAN
in
HEAVEN

〰〰〰

Sophia and the
New Star Wisdom

Robert Powell

THE SIGN
of the
SON OF MAN
in
HEAVEN

*Sophia
and the
New Star Wisdom*

SOPHIA FOUNDATION PRESS

SAN RAFAEL, CALIFORNIA

Second, rev. and expanded edition,
Sophia Foundation Press, 2007
First edition, Sun Cross Press, 1999
© Robert Powell 2007

For information, address:
Sophia Foundation Press, P.O. Box 151011
San Rafael, California 94915, USA

Library of Congress Cataloging-in-Publication Data

Powell, Robert, 1947–
The sign of the Son of man in Heaven:
Sophia and the new star wisdom. — Second, expanded, ed.

p. cm.

Rev. ed. of: The sign of the Son of Man in the heavens.
Includes bibliographical references.
ISBN 978 1 59731 159 5 (pbk: alk. paper)
ISBN 978 1 59731 161 8 (hardcover: alk. paper)
1. Astrology. 2. Zodiac. 3. Wisdom—Religious aspects.
4. Jesus Christ—New Age movement interpretations.
I. Powell, Robert, 1947– Sign of the Son of Man in the heavens. II. Title.
BF1711.P747 2007
133.5—dc22   2007026532

CONTENTS

Foreword

to the Second Edition

THE SIGN OF THE SON OF MAN IN THE HEAVENS is identified in this book with the location of the vernal point in
Aquarius. The vernal point will leave Pisces and enter Aquarius in
2375, and at this time the Age of Aquarius will begin—lasting for
2,160 years until 4535, when the Age of Capricorn will begin.

Exact dating of the astrological ages is possible now that the original definition of the zodiac—as defined by the Babylonians—has
been recovered, enabling the original zodiac to be restored in its
entirety, as I have done in *History of the Zodiac*, the book of my
Ph.D. thesis. Thereby the unfolding of the zodiacal ages is placed on
a secure historical basis and a new sense of cosmic time is made
possible—that is, a sense for participating, through a living astronomy, with the unfolding of cosmic evolution as measured by the
slow but steady movement of the vernal point backwards through
the zodiacal signs (known as the 'precession of the equinoxes').

It has to be borne in mind that all the ancient cultures looked up
to and were guided by the stars. A most striking example is offered
by the achievements of Polynesian sailors in their canoes who navi-
gated their way across the Pacific from Tahiti to Hawaii—a distance
of more than 2,500 miles (over 4,000 kilometers)—guided by the
stars. It was particularly the fact that Arcturus (Hawaiian
Hokule'a—'star of joy') culminates above the Hawaiian Islands as
the zenith star that enabled these intrepid sailors to navigate their
way. For the return journey to Tahiti they were guided by Sirius
(Hawaian *Hokuho'okelewa'a*—'canoe-guiding star'), which is the
zenith star of Tahiti.

It is clear from this example and many others—the astronomical
observatories (stone circles such as Stonehenge) of the Druids, the

alignment of temples and pyramids to various stars in ancient Egypt, and so on—that humanity in ancient times lived in attunement with the cosmos. What happened historically to hinder this attunement?

The close relationship with the starry heavens was impeded by the new focus that came with Greek astronomy, which emphasized the Sun as providing the frame of reference for their celestial observations. A prime example is the Greek astronomer Ptolemy, who introduced the tropical zodiac (relating to the Sun's path rather than to the stars) into astrology around AD 150. Since then, gradually, humanity's living relationship with the starry heavens receded and in our time is virtually non-existent. Having lost our connection to the world of stars, it is now time to re-awaken to the stellar world and find a conscious connection to the stars. The sign of the Son of Man in the heavens is beckoning to us to take this step, so that a new and living star wisdom (Astrosophy) can arise. Hence the subtitle to this book: *Sophia and the New Star Wisdom.*

This book of six lectures that I held in 1993 serves as an excellent introduction to the new star wisdom (Astrosophy) and is as helpful now that it is republished in a second edition as it was when it first appeared.

For those who would like to follow up and deepen into Astrosophy further, the following books that I have written are all available through the Sophia Foundation or directly from Sophia Foundation Press (in the case of the *History of the Zodiac* from Sophia Academic Press).

History of the Zodiac

In this study the sidereal zodiac is restored to its rightful place as the original zodiac, tracing it back to the Babylonians in the fifth century BC. The fruit of thirty years of research, this book is intended not only for scholars but for general readers as well, and offers the clearest and most comprehensive study of the history of the zodiac yet published.

Hermetic Astrology I: Astrology and Reincarnation

Includes a comprehensive basis for a new science of karmic astrology, specific reincarnation examples, the astrology of the ancient Babylonians and Egyptians, the New Age, the Second Coming of Christ, and more.

Hermetic Astrology II: Astrological Biography

Presents a detailed look at embryonic life, conception to birth, in relation to the unfolding of destiny in human biography through seven-year periods and also includes a study of historical examples of karmic relationships, the esoteric significance of the outer planets, working with the lunar rhythms in meditation, and much more—including astrological biographies of Richard Wagner and Rudolf Steiner.

Christian Hermetic Astrology:
the Star of the Magi and the Life of Christ

Consisting of discourses set in the 'Temple of the Sun', where Hermes and his pupils gather to meditate on the cosmic aspects of the birth, miracles, and passion of Jesus Christ, this book outlines a modern path of the magi leading to a Christian star wisdom.

Chronicle of the Living Christ, the Life and Ministry
of Jesus Christ: Foundations of Cosmic Christianity

Based on the visions of Anne Catherine Emmerich, this foundational work includes a day by day chronicle of the three and a half year ministry of Jesus Christ with horoscopes of the birth and death of Jesus, Mary, and John the Baptist, and events in the life of Christ.

The Christ Mystery: Reflections on the Second Coming

The fruit of many years reflection on the Second Coming and it's cosmological aspects, this work looks at the approaching trial of humanity, and the challenges of living in apocalyptic times, against the background of 'great signs from heaven'.

The Christian Star Calendar

Published yearly in October of the preceding year, this publication is a guide to the ongoing correspondences of Christ's life found in the stellar and etheric world and includes articles of topical interest as well as a complete sidereal ephemeris and aspectarian, geocentric and heliocentric, for the year.

Introduction to Christian Star Calendar

This is a guide to working with the *Christian Star Calendar* on a daily basis, including information on mega stars, the 36 decans, and many other topics.

Cosmic Dances of the Planets
(written together with Lacquanna Paul)

This study material describes the seven classical planets and their forms and gestures in cosmic dance, with diagrams, including a wealth of information on the planets.

Cosmic Dances of the Zodiac
(written together with Lacquanna Paul)

This study material describes the twelve signs in relation to the stars, provides meditation material and outlines the zodiacal forms and gestures in cosmic dance, with diagrams, and new research on the 36 decans and 12 zodiacal signs.

The Most Holy Trinosophia
and the New Revelation of the Divine Feminine

This book discusses Sophia as a Trinity—Mother, Daughter, and Holy Soul—and as the feminine aspect of the Godhead, and includes an Introduction to the Divine Feminine by Daniel Andreev, author of *The Rose of the World*, and a Foreword by Carol Parrish, founder of Sancta Sophia Seminary.

The Sophia Teachings

This book is also available as a set of six audiocassettes produced by Sounds True. It unveils and embraces the 'Mother of all humanity' and surveys Christianity's mystical past as well as the Greek philosophers, King Solomon, Hildegard of Bingen, the Russian Sophiologists, Sophia's influence on the foundations of civilization, and more. The book includes additional material on the Virgin of Guadalupe.

Elijah Come Again: A Study in Reincarnation
(with Lacquanna Paul)

A study of the Elijah individuality in various incarnations, with horoscope comparisons from one life to the next. The book culminates with an appraisal of the significance of this great individuality in our time as a herald of the Second Coming of Christ.

The Astrological Revolution
(with Kevin Dann—in preparation)

This book explores in depth the pros and cons of using the tropical and sidereal zodiacs in astrology. Starting with the secure foundation of the rules of astrological reincarnation, the astrological revolution is a result of the application of these rules, analogous to the astronomical revolution that took place as a result of the discovery of the laws of planetary motion early in the seventeenth century.

Acknowledgments

To all seekers of star wisdom, especially Willi Sucher (1902–1985), who encouraged me to research the mysteries of the world of stars.

◈

The lectures that form the basis of this book were given at a conference in North Vancouver, British Columbia, in July 1993. They have been revised and expanded for this second edition.

Toward a New
Wisdom of the Stars

A FIRST IMPRESSION OF VANCOUVER, between the water
on the one side and the mountains on the other, reminds
us of various scenes depicted in the Gospels. Christ often taught at
the water's edge or even on a boat addressing people on the shore.
Many other scenes are described in which he went up on to a mountain and taught there. These two different qualities come together
here in Vancouver. We could say the watery element is more connected with an imaginative quality. And going up into the mountains, one feels the purity of the air; it is the quality of inspiration—
breathing in spirituality—that one finds in the mountains. These
two qualities of imagination and inspiration seem to be living here
in Vancouver, at least as a potential to be developed.

As will emerge during the course of our meeting together, the
West Coast is, I believe, very significant for the future. Important
spiritual impulses will unfold here. It is a privilege to be here on the
West Coast of Canada and to work together in developing a new
wisdom of the stars. This is a task many people have worked with
and continue to work with. In this connection one person I would
like to mention, who also came to Vancouver, is Willi Sucher. I was
privileged to meet him and work together with him. He came from
Germany to Britain before World War II. Around 1960 he moved
from England to California. His life was dedicated to developing
astrosophy, a new wisdom of the stars. He felt that the Western
world is the place for the founding of a new star wisdom. Central to
his work was the opening up of a consciousness of the Christ
Impulse in relation to the stars, especially the three years of Christ's
ministry between the Baptism in the Jordan and the Mystery of
Golgotha. This focusing upon the Christ Impulse is essential for the

development of a new wisdom of the stars, and we shall look at this more closely during the course of these days together.

When one looks at what is now practiced as astrology, this actually has very little to do with the ancient wisdom of the stars. What does one think of in contemplating the human being's relationship to the stars? Nowadays there is a tendency to focus upon the horoscope at the moment of birth. Modern astrology works almost exclusively with this. But this is only one aspect of what star wisdom is about. Astrosophy is something all-embracing, encompassing every aspect of life, our relationship to the spiritual world and our relationship to the Earth. So we are not going to be looking at horoscopes during this time together, but rather shall try to broaden our understanding of the human being's relationship to the cosmos.

The new star wisdom arising in our time is a metamorphosis of the ancient star wisdom. Thus, it is helpful to look back historically to see what happened to the ancient wisdom of the stars. It flourished above all in the ancient civilizations of Egypt and Babylon. For example, the Babylonian priesthood practiced stargazing—gazing up to the stars—and the priests received messages through dreams, through inspiration from divine beings whom they saw as connected with the stars. It was their task to bring what they received as divine inspiration to the king, who was expected to direct the affairs of the country on the basis of this communion with the world of stars. The whole of Babylonian civilization was directed out of this communion with the world of stars, especially with the seven planetary gods. When they looked up to the Sun, the Babylonians did not see it simply as a ball of gas emitting light and warmth. They saw the Sun as the dwelling-place of a divine being whom they called *Shamash*; and that of the Moon they called *Sin*. Mercury they saw as the dwelling-place of the divine being *Nebo*, the scribe of the gods, who holds the tablets of destiny in his hands. And Venus they saw as the abode of the divine being *Ishtar*, the consort of the leader of the divine pantheon. This leadership they saw connected with the divine being of Jupiter, whom they called *Marduk*; and in connection with Saturn they saw the god *Ninib*. For the Babylonians each of these divine beings possessed certain characteristics. For example, the god of Mars, *Nergal*, they saw as aggressive, as needing to be appeased so that there would not be war and destruction. Babylonian religious life entailed observance of the cosmic world.

One of the tasks of the Babylonian priesthood was to write cuneiform texts—one of the earliest kinds of languages, written by pressing a stylus into clay. These texts were preserved for thousands of years. At the end of nineteenth century and the beginning of the twentieth, these texts were excavated and have been to a large extent translated. So now we know much about the life of this ancient civilization. For example, we know that the Babylonians were the first to develop what may be called a scientific approach: from their clairvoyant experiences of the cosmic world they were able to relate to what can be measured and described in scientific terms. This development extended over many centuries.

A very special development took place in the sixth century BC, which was a remarkable turning-point in time. In fact, in many different countries a tremendous new impulse came in around 600 BC. There was the development of Greek philosophy through the emergence of the Greek philosophers; the appearance of Buddha in India; and the development of the scientific impulse of the Babylonians. This time around 600 BC denotes the beginning of the previous Age of Michael, a special historical period that lasted up until the time of Plato and Aristotle during which a new kind of culture on the level of thinking was developed. This was the time of the birth of philosophy, and here the ancient star wisdom began to disappear. A living communion with the world of stars receded and what came in its place was more and more the development of an astronomy and astrology based on calculating the movements of the planets and utilizing these calculations for the computation of horoscopes. Looking at this development, we see that 'astrosophia', the wisdom of the stars (*sophia* means wisdom, *astro* relates to the stars) passed over into *philosophia* (*philosophia*—the love of *sophia*, divine wisdom). This was a new development from 600 BC onward, whereby the faculty of human intelligence became more and more significant. Up until that point in time, there was not really any intellectual culture, apart from a few isolated examples. Following the transition from astrosophia to philosophia, the impulse of philosophy has remained of central importance for the whole of Western civilization. The works of Plato and Aristotle have been significant 'guiding lights' for the development of culture here in the West.

Let us now take a big jump to the year 1879, toward the end of the nineteenth century, that is, the beginning of a new Age of Michael. Here again something new entered in. Theosophy, the 'wisdom of God', was born around this time, and shortly after, through Rudolf Steiner, the birth of anthroposophy (this word literally means 'wisdom of man', and we shall enter more deeply into this point later). Thus, there took place a development over centuries from astrosophy to philosophy to anthroposophy. Rudolf Steiner described the reason for choosing the word anthroposophy when he spoke at the founding of the Anthroposophical Society in 1913. He indicated the development from philosophy to anthroposophy, speaking of how the word philosophy originally meant 'love of the divine wisdom'. For example, he referred to the poet Dante, almost as if Dante was in love with the being of Sophia, the personification of the divine wisdom. There was still a feeling for the being of Sophia right up to the Middle Ages, at least up to the time of Dante (1265–1321). Then followed the development of modern science, which arose from the time of the Renaissance onward. And a deeper feeling for Sophia, who had been central to the whole of philosophy, faded more and more into the background.

Among the first modern philosophers was the French thinker Descartes (1596–1650), who placed at the center of his philosophy, "I think, therefore I am." This was something quite new, in that Descartes placed himself at the center of his philosophy rather than relating to the divine wisdom. In Rudolf Steiner's characterization of this development, he describes how the being of Sophia 'died' in the human being. What was previously the divine wisdom weaving into philosophy became more and more a purely human affair. Sophia, having poured herself out, 'died' into the human being—sacrificing herself so that human beings could begin to think for themselves, to experience their thoughts as their own thoughts. Now, however, with the start of the New Age that we have entered since the end of the nineteenth century, we have the task of bringing Sophia alive within us—and this signifies the birth of anthroposophia, the new wisdom that arises when the being of Sophia is resurrected within the human being. She is part of the essence of human existence and will appear more and more to human beings as an objective being who will lead us into the future. This is central to the theme of our gathering here. We are approaching the time when Sophia, the divine wisdom, will become a being to whom we can relate, so that we can speak of the coming of a Sophianic period in history. This is connected with the approaching Age of Aquarius, during which the being of Sophia will become more and more active in the shaping of all culture. Anthroposophy is leading us toward this future age of Sophia. We see, then, a development through the ages leading to the future revelation of Sophia, which will include a new cosmology, a new star wisdom, a new astrosophia. What we are seeking is to experience within ourselves the birth of seed impulses for the future, for the arising of a new culture. For Sophia is the heart of all true culture, all true science, all true art, all true religion; and the quest to find this heart of culture is the search for the Divine Sophia, who through the development of modern science since the time of the Renaissance has more and more receded from human consciousness.

In the Middle Ages there was still a living consciousness of Sophia. She was looked upon especially as Patroness of the Arts, and there are representations of her inspiring architecture, sculpture, music, poetry, painting, and drama. Against this background we can understand something of what was living in Dante, one of the greatest poets of the Middle Ages: his poetry was written out of a great love for Sophia. For him, this was philosophy. Within anthro-posophy, too, there lives an impulse for the renewal of the arts. Anthroposophy begins as science (spiritual science, a new way of understanding the world), evolves to become art, and culminates in giving birth to a new religious experience of the world. The role art plays is something central to the opening-up of new faculties, new qualities of the heart that can relate to the Divine Sophia. Especially through the art of eurythmy, born out of anthroposophy, a path to a new relationship to Sophia and a new star wisdom is possible. Eurythmy can be a great help in opening up new faculties within us.

For this, nobody need feel they should have any gift with regard to movement, for every human being able to move his limbs can enter into the spirit of eurythmy, which has come to birth in the present Age of Pisces but which really belongs to the future Age of Aquarius. Eurythmy will evolve in the future, but the seed impulse for eurythmy had to be given so that it would be possible to work with eurythmy now to develop it for the future.

Something similar is evident in the case of the birth of music. Several hundred centuries before Christ, Orpheus incarnated in Greece and brought the impulse for the development of music. This developed on a primitive level with the Greeks (primitive in comparison with what we now call music), but these modest beginnings inaugurated by Orpheus were necessary for the later more sophisticated evolution. Down through the centuries from the time of Orpheus music then underwent a further development within the Church. The Church carried music through the centuries following the coming of Christ. Then, at the end of the seventeenth century, a tremendous new impulse came in. This was the birth of the sophisticated music that came about through the great composers: Bach, Haydn, Mozart, Beethoven, and the great Romantic composers— something on a very high and profound level! All of this, however, needed the seed impulses that were laid thousands of years before, through Orpheus.

Orpheus was not only a musical genius; he was also a great dancer. Orpheus and Musaeus were regarded as two great dancers in the tradition of sacred dance of Greek civilization. It is the same with eurythmy, for here too it is a matter of something present now only in seed form, in rudimentary form, that in the course of centuries will develop into something that will lead human beings into a new communion with nature and with the cosmic world. There is the possibility, through eurythmy, of opening up new faculties. Eurythmy is a metamorphosis, a rebirth of the ancient temple dance that was practiced in the Egyptian mysteries and in the temples of Ancient Greece. It is possible to enter into the spirit of eurythmy as a rebirth of the ancient temple dance.

Let us now look more closely at the other art that will play an important role for us, the art of music. Music, too, has the possibility of opening up spiritual faculties and bringing us into communion with higher worlds. This is the case whenever we hear true music—music born out of the higher worlds. True music is a reflection of the divine music that in the ancient mysteries was called the harmonies of the spheres. The movements of the planets on their paths resound. As Goethe says in the opening words of his great drama *Faust*, "The Sun resounds as in days of yore." This was an experience in the ancient mysteries, at a certain level, of the opening of spiritual faculties: the hearing of the cosmic realm, of the harmonies of the spheres. Even before the birth of music as we know it through Orpheus, and later through Pythagoras, even prior to this, the hearing of the harmonies of the spheres was central to the initiation undergone in the Egyptian mysteries. On the one hand the temple dance reflected the movements of the planets; on the other, there was the content of the initiation itself. Through this initiation human beings experienced themselves outside the body and in the presence of an exalted spiritual being whom they called Isis, who was actually the same as Sophia. In this initiation there was an experience of being in the presence of Isis. There sounded forth from her music and divine words—resounding words. The quest for Sophia in our time is also a search for the re-experiencing of the harmonies of the spheres. The great composers were those human beings able to carry over something of a reflection of the divine music. Their music is a kind of frozen manifestation of the movements of the planets in the sounding of the harmonies of the spheres.

The Greeks spoke of the lyre of Orpheus, or the lyre of Apollo, or the lyre of Hermes. The lyre is a stringed instrument. There are seven tones in the lyre of Orpheus, and these seven tones, according to the Pythagoreans, correspond to the seven planets. For them there was a direct relationship between music and the cosmos. All of this has been largely forgotten, but for those in the Greek mystery schools it was known that the seven tones in the scale are connected with the seven planets. Various scales or modes were developed in Greek music, and these were taken over in modified form in early church music. The impulse went further within the church. One important development in the Middle Ages was the creation of musical notation, through which it became possible to write music down. There was also the development of Gregorian chant. Subsequently, there arose within church music the great composers such as Palestrina and Monteverdi in Italy. In Germany and elsewhere, some people began to think about the inconsistencies between the different scales or modes in church music. In 1697 the German musician Andreas Werkmeister published for the first time a system for relating the scales or keys together in one system. Directly after the publication of Werkmeister's work, Johann Sebastian Bach adopted this system, incorporating it in his *Well-tempered Clavier.* This system is based no longer on seven, as in Greek music, but on twelve. The system elaborated by Bach encompasses twelve major and twelve minor keys. Bach composed forty-eight preludes and fugues, two for each major and minor key, signifying a completely new development in the history of music: the development of a twelvefold system in place of the earlier sevenfold system.

Eurythmy, as most of you will know, is many-sided, and two of its aspects are *speech* eurythmy, which is movement to recited poetry, to the spoken word, and *tone* eurythmy, which is movement to music. One of the first tone eurythmists, the Dutch woman Hendrika Hollenbach, was told by Rudolf Steiner that the twelve major and twelve minor keys are connected with the twelve signs of the zodiac. Professor Herman Beckh took up this indication and worked it out in detail. Beckh, who was a professor of sanskrit and oriental languages, was known for his many books on the history of oriental religions, including works on Buddhism and on Zoroastrianism. Beckh also became a priest of the Christian Community. He was deeply interested in music, and set about investigating the qualities of the twelve major and twelve minor keys in connection with the twelve signs of the zodiac. This is very significant, because on the one hand it opens up for us a new appreciation of music, and on the other it enables us to find a new connection with the cosmos. By way of analogy with the Greeks, Orpheus brought the impulse of music utilizing a lyre with seven tones, and it was only later that the Pythagoreans related the seven tones to the seven planets. Similarly, just as the Greeks had the lyre of Orpheus, so we now have the *Well-tempered Clavier* of Johann Sebastian Bach. Later, through an indication of Rudolf Steiner, worked out by

Herman Beckh, the relationship of this to the twelve signs of the zodiac was established.

I have indicated here the basis of this correspondence between the twelve major and minor keys and the twelve signs of the zodiac. If we begin with the major keys, the start of the circle is C major.

Figure 1

*Correspondence of the twelve major and minor keys
with the twelve signs of the zodiac*

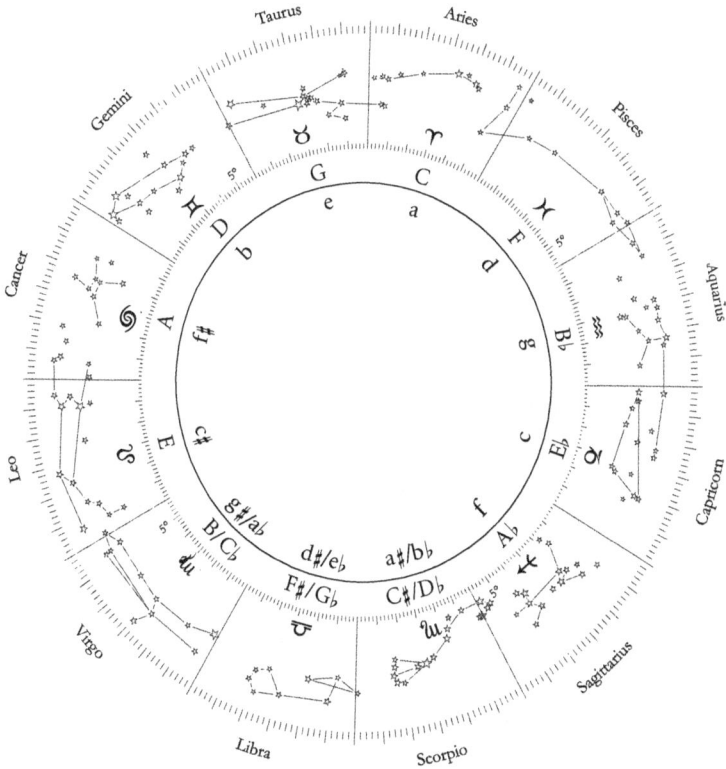

major—outer circle; minor—inner circle

Looking at the circular apparent orbit of the Sun through the zodiacal signs during the course of one year, ascent signifies an increase in light. In the same way, proceeding around the circle of keys, we go from C major to G major. In G major we have a lightening-up of the key. This becomes intensified as we move to the next key, D major, which corresponds to Gemini. It becomes lighter still and reaches a high point with A major, connected with Cancer. Going further, the correspondences are: E major in connection with Leo; B major with Virgo. We cross a boundary or threshold when we come to F-sharp major, which corresponds to Libra. Here we enter into a different mood. For example, the compositions of Mozart are mainly in keys on the ascending side (top half of circle on page 9), whereas a romantic composer like Chopin preferred keys on the descending side (lower half of circle on page 9). On the basis of these cosmic-musical correspondences, we have the possibility of arriving at a new understanding of music. Of course, this applies only to the great composers who incarnated on the Earth after this new step inaugurated by Bach. They were able to work with this system as part of a profound intuitive connection with the whole realm of the harmonies of the spheres.

For example, if we look at the works of Mozart, we find an inner consistency in his utilization of the keys. As many of you will know, Mozart was both a devoted Catholic and a dedicated Freemason. He composed several works for his brother Masons, and many of these are in the key of E-flat major, which is the deepest one here, connected with Capricorn. These works have a cultic, majestic, celebratory quality, and we can feel a connection with Capricorn, which is the deepest time of year within the whole cycle of the Sun. It is the midnight Sun, when the Sun is working in its most spiritual and hidden way. This helps us understand how, through an intuitive knowledge of these things, Mozart came to compose these Masonic works in the key of E-flat major. Works that he composed in C major, corresponding to Aries, are usually very bright and have a wonderful clarity resounding through them, whereas works he composed in G major, corresponding to Taurus, have a lightness and joyfulness, celebrating the mysteries of nature. Works he composed in D major have a note of victory, of triumph, that shines through. Here the Sun rises higher to reveal its glory in the sign of Gemini. Then, coming round to the high point in Cancer, works he composed in A major have a light-filled and playful quality. These remarks are based upon a work by Aloys Greither,[1] who studied Mozart's works in relation to the twelve major and twelve minor keys.

Coming now to Herman Beckh, it was he who originally took up this correspondence of the twelve major and twelve minor keys with the twelve signs of the zodiac. He sought to objectively describe musical qualities. He was a great lover of the works of the composer Richard Wagner, and in Wagner's operas he saw the possibility of finding this more objective description of musical qualities, because of the combination of music and the spoken word that is connected with the unfolding of the content of the opera. Herman Beckh went through all Wagner's major operas and found that very often where Wagner wanted to express something dark and threatening he used the key of D-flat major, which corresponds to Scorpio. Or if he wanted to express the quality of looking into the future with hope and a sense of redemption, a feeling for something new on the horizon, he often composed in the key of B-flat major, corresponding to Aquarius. In his work (which as far as I know is not translated into English: *The Language of the Keys*),[2] Beckh uses primarily the works of Wagner as his basis, but he draws also upon the whole classical tradition from Johann Sebastian Bach up to and including Anton Bruckner. He also makes it clear that his thesis applies only to the great composers, those who were able to work with the 12 major and 12 minor keys in a creative way.

There is a CD with a selection of two series of piano pieces going through the twelve keys.[3] In the second series, all twelve pieces are in the major keys, except for the Leo piece by Schubert, which is in the key of C-sharp minor. The minor keys are shown in the inner

1. Aloys Greither, *Wolfgang Amadé Mozart* (Rowohlt Taschenbuch Verlag, 1962).

2. Hermann Beckh, *Die Sprache der Tonarten* (Stuttgart: Verlag Urachhaus, 1937).

3. Ludmila Gricenko, *Zodiac Music* CD with twenty-four pieces, two for each sign of the zodiac, available from the Sophia Foundation of North America, www.sophiafoundation.org. The music recorded on this CD is part of the repertoire of music in the Choreocosmos School of Cosmic and Sacred Dance for the work with zodiac in the cosmic dance of eurythmy. A way of working with these

circle in the figure on page 9. These are the so-called 'relative keys' to the major keys. In general, they have a quality of sadness. With the major keys the tendency is more one of a joyful quality. What we can hear or experience with this piece by Schubert in C-sharp minor is that it has the Leo quality of longing, a heart quality of longing. This same quality we find also in another work in C-sharp minor, one of the most famous piano works—Beethoven's *Moonlight Sonata*. Herman Beckh describes this quality in terms of a 'midsummer night's dream'. If we think of a warm summer night, we can feel something of this Leo quality.

twenty-four pieces in cosmic dance—including the choreographies and the eurythmy gestures and sounds for the twelve zodiacal signs—is described in Lacquanna Paul and Robert Powell, *Cosmic Dances of the Zodiac* (San Rafael, CA: Sophia Foundation Press, 2007).

The Zodiac

THE NEW REVELATION OF SOPHIA coming in the Age of Aquarius will be a tremendous spiritual impulse for the rebuilding and reshaping of culture, through which new impulses of community will arise. The Sophianic impulse worked through the ages from the ancient astrosophia or star wisdom of Egypt and Babylon, through the period of philosophy, the age of Greece and Rome. And in our time, with the impulse of theosophy and anthroposophy, we take a step toward the future, toward the coming revelation of Sophia. Our work together in developing a new wisdom of the stars—through music, through eurythmy, through coming to a new understanding of humanity's relationship with the cosmos—is a preparation for this new revelation of Sophia.

As already referred to, in the history of music—for the Greeks, and continuing on through church music—the focus was on the seven tones, which the Pythagoreans saw in relation to the seven planets. In the seventeenth and eighteenth centuries a breakthrough came with the development of the system of twelve major and twelve minor keys, elaborated by Johann Sebastian Bach in the *Well-tempered Clavier*, which laid the foundation for the development of the great works of the classical and romantic tradition. In the twentieth century we have seen the development of twelve-tone music, overthrowing the cosmically-based system of the twelve major and twelve minor keys. One writer in Germany has likened this introduction through Arnold Schoenberg of the twelve-tone system to the communist revolution, whereby the cosmic order of music of the classical tradition has been threatened. However, just as there have been many positive things in the Eastern communist countries despite communism, so one could also say there have been many wonderful works composed in twelve-tone music *despite* this twelve-tone system. Now it seems that some composers are returning to the classical tone system. One significant step is to become conscious of the correspondence in the classical system of the keys with the signs of the zodiac. This can give rise to a completely new relationship to classical music. And this can be intensified still further through eurythmy. The step from the seven-fold system to the twelve-fold system is characteristic of an evolutionary step for the whole of humanity. It is indicative of the fact that we are called upon to come to an understanding of twelvefoldness; so now let us turn to the zodiac with its twelve signs.

During the course of the twentieth century we have seen renewed interest in the signs of the zodiac. However, there is little understanding of what the zodiac actually is. As referred to earlier, the previous Age of Michael began in the sixth century BC. These are special historical ages, each lasting about 350 years. Toward the end of the nineteenth century, in 1879, a new Age of Michael began. With this came the possibility of a new opening-up of spiritual faculties, as had also been the case in the sixth century BC at the start of the last Age of Michael. And as mentioned already, there was at that time the impulse of the Buddha in India, of Pythagoras and the Greek philosophers in Greece; and in Babylon itself a special development took place. Now, no development happens of itself; human beings (or at least one human being) always stand behind it.

In fact, in the sixth century BC a great initiate was incarnated in Babylon. As an initiate, he was comparable to, or even higher than, Moses, who accomplished so much for the people of Israel; and he was still higher than Hermes, who accomplished so much for the culture of Egypt. This individuality living in Babylon is the individuality known to the Greeks as Zoroaster and known to the Babylonian priesthood as Zaratas. Zoroaster was actually of Persian descent and was related to the Persian king Cyrus the Great. As we know from the Bible, the sixth century BC was the time of the Jewish captivity in Babylon. In 586 BC, Nebuchadnezzar II conquered Jerusalem and took a large number of the people of Israel to Babylon into captivity. As described in the book of Ezra, "The Lord took the hand of Cyrus and led him to free His people." This is exactly what happened. Cyrus the Great rose from relative obscurity to become the head of a huge army that conquered one land after the other, establishing a vast empire; and in 539 BC Cyrus conquered Babylon. Many of you will know of the painting by Rembrandt showing the scene of King Belshazzar (the son of Nebuchadnezzar II) in Babylon, drinking from—and thus desecrating—the sacred vessels of the temple in Jerusalem. There then appeared the writing on the wall which said "God has numbered the days of your kingdom and brought it to an end." That very night Cyrus the Great conquered Babylon. King Belshazzar was slain and so the dynasty of the Babylonian kings came to an end. Zoroaster (Zaratas) came to Babylon in the wake of the conquest of the city by Cyrus.

Cyrus the Great was renowned for his great tolerance. In the different countries he conquered, he allowed the spiritual traditions and customs of the countries to continue. In Babylon also the priests were permitted to continue their ancient rites centered around the worship of the planetary pantheon under the leadership of Marduk. The central place of worship was the holy temple of Esagila in Babylon. Here was Marduk's sanctuary. The Persian prophet Zaratas was recognized by the Babylonian priesthood as a great initiate. He taught the priesthood and brought them knowledge of the zodiac. Here, for the first time in the history of humanity, arose a scientific definition of the zodiac.[1]

What does the word 'zodiac' mean? It comes from the Greek *Zoa*—living creature. 'Zodiac' means the circle of living creatures. If we look up to the starry constellations—the twelve constellations of the zodiac—we see the different stars. For example, looking up to Leo we see the shining star Regulus, the heart of the Lion, or looking up to Virgo, we see Spica, the ear of corn held by the Virgin. This was already known to the Babylonian priesthood. Zoroaster taught that the shining stars are an outer revelation, the 'body' of exalted spiritual beings. Just as human beings have a physical body, these beings manifest their body as the groupings of the constellations of stars. Zoroaster referred to these as 'holy living creatures'. This was part of his teaching.

---

1. Robert Powell, *History of the Zodiac* (San Rafael, CA: Sophia Academic Press, 2007), traces the history of the definition of the zodiac.

Zoroaster was also able to communicate the 'sphere of influence' of each of these twelve great beings, the twelve holy living creatures. His impulse signified a carrying-over from clairvoyance into a scientific definition—that is, something that can be comprehended and measured. The great achievement of Zoroaster in Babylon was the defining of the sphere of influence of the zodiac. Referring to twelve signs in the heavens, he indicated the sphere of influence of the twelve holy creatures who manifest themselves through the twelve signs, and indicated that they each have an equal influence extending through 30 degrees. Together the twelve signs make up 360 degrees, with the star Aldebaran, the 'Bull's Eye' in the middle of Taurus, marking the middle of the sign of Taurus. It was central to his teaching that the star Aldebaran is located in the middle of Taurus. The sign of Taurus comprises the Pleiades, Aldebaran and the Hyades, and also the horns of the Bull in such a way that Aldebaran is at 15 degrees of Taurus. This places the little star cluster of the Pleiades at 5 degrees Taurus. Opposite, on the other side of the zodiac, is the constellation of the Scorpion. According to Zoroaster, the bright star Antares marks the middle of the Scorpion and is thus at 15 degrees Scorpio. Antares is the Heart of the Scorpion; Aldebaran is the Bull's Eye. Having identified these two stars as situated at the center (15 degrees) of their respective signs, it was possible to locate the positions of all the other stars in the zodiac. For example the Lion's Heart, Regulus, is located at 5 degrees Leo, and Spica, the Ear of Corn held by the Virgin, is at 29 degrees Virgo, etc. This was the original definition of the zodiac. A Babylonian star catalogue has been excavated giving the longitudes of many of the stars in this system,[2] as have also hundreds of cuneiform tablets showing the positions of the planets in the signs of the zodiac, all bearing witness to the use by the Babylonians of the ancient original zodiac now called the sidereal zodiac.

It is important to bear in mind that this is not an abstract definition of the zodiac. It was born out of clairvoyant vision, on the basis of an actual perception of the working of exalted spiritual beings. Some indication of this vision is given in the Book of Revelation by

2. Ibid., Appendix I.

St John where, in Chapter Four, he describes a vision of the holy living creatures around the throne of God: the first living creature like a lion (Leo), the second living creature like an ox (Taurus), the third living creature with a human face (corresponding to Aquarius), and the fourth living creature like a flying eagle (this being the vision of Scorpio, which in earlier times was seen as an eagle)[3]. Again, the same vision of the four holy living creatures manifesting through these four zodiacal signs is described in the Book of Ezekiel. Ezekiel describes these holy living creatures and calls them 'Cherubim'. He says that these beings bear the throne of God. The Old Testament prophet Ezekiel, Zoroaster in Babylon, and St John the Divine each experienced the holy living creatures who work through the zodiac.

In our century too, Rudolf Steiner had this vision, which he describes in his lectures on the spiritual hierarchies. There he also answers the question why St John and Ezekiel describe only four of the holy living creatures rather than the full circle of twelve. He says that the four so-called 'fixed signs' of Taurus, Leo, Scorpio (Eagle), and Aquarius (Waterman) stood out more strongly to the clairvoyants of antiquity. Closer clairvoyant vision shows that each of these four holy living creatures is flanked on each side by two other holy living creatures. Thus the holy living creature manifesting as the Ox or Bull is flanked on the one side by the Ram and on the other by the Twins. So it is with each of the four, giving a circle of twelve. It is interesting that in the Persian tradition, with which Zoroaster was associated, royal watcher stars are spoken of, those royal stars being: Aldebaran in the middle of Taurus, Antares in the middle of Scorpio, Regulus the heart of the Lion, and Fomalhaut, the star in the stream of water pouring forth from the urn of the Waterman and marking the Southern Fish. Hence these four signs, with their royal stars, also stood out in the tradition. Rudolf Steiner referred to this majestic vision of the Cherubim. He said that these twelve holy living creatures have been at work throughout the whole of creation

---

3. Robert Powell, *Christian Hermetic Astrology: The Star of the Magi and the Life of Christ* (Gt. Barrington, MA: SteinerBooks, 1998), pp 162–163, describes the metamorphosis from the Eagle to the Scorpion.

since the beginning, going back to the time of ancient Saturn, and especially during the time of ancient Saturn. According to him, it is not just the Cherubim that work through the twelve zodiacal constellations, but the whole of the first hierarchy of spiritual beings. These are the beings known in Jewish tradition as Seraphim, Cherubim, and Thrones. Looking up to the zodiacal constellations, outwardly we see in the stars the 'bodies' of these spiritual beings—who are the highest spiritual beings, closest to the Holy Trinity of the Father, the Son and the Holy Spirit. These divine beings receive impulses from the Holy Trinity and ray them down to the Earth. Here there is an outpouring of divine love of the Seraphim, divine wisdom of the Cherubim, and divine will of the Thrones. The Hebrew word *seraphim* can be translated as 'fiery love'. These highest beings, the Seraphim, spirits of divine love, burn with love of the Holy Trinity. These impulses are taken up by the Cherubim. The word *cherubim* means in Jewish tradition the spirits who are 'flowing over with wisdom'. They are wise and their wisdom is poured out. They are assisted by the Thrones, who stream out forces of will. The word *throne* conjures up an image of an exalted seat of a majestic being executing divine will. What rays down upon the Earth from the twelve signs of the zodiac, from the circle of holy living creatures, are impulses of love, wisdom, and will.

As was said earlier, in ancient Babylon Zoroaster had the task of translating knowledge of the zodiac into a scientific definition. This he accomplished, resulting in the sidereal zodiac. Our task now is to go in the other direction, to start from the scientific level (i.e., a new scientific understanding of the zodiac) and to go beyond this, to penetrate to the mystical dimension underlying the signs of the zodiac, that is, to the spiritual beings who are at work in the direction and guidance of cosmic evolution. This is our task in coming to a new understanding of the zodiac, and at the same time to realize that what is characterized in astrology as the birth horoscope is the human being's relationship with higher spiritual beings. What is often characterized in modern astrology in trivial terms, actually refers to something very deep and profound.

What lay behind the impulse of Zoroaster to translate a spiritual perception of the zodiac, arising from his initiation, into a scientific form—from which the whole development of Babylonian astronomy and astrology followed? First of all the zodiac had to be defined, so that the Babylonian priests could begin to write down their observations of the movements of the planets against the background of the zodiacal signs. Recording all of this, they arrived at a scientific understanding of the laws of the movements of the planets. For example, they came to understand that the planet Venus has an eight-year cycle from which they could accurately predict the movements of Venus, and that Saturn has a 29½ year cycle, and so on. What underlay the step from spiritual perception to scientific knowledge? It was to make preparation for the future. We cannot really understand this step in isolation. It needs to be seen in relation to the fact that there was at the same time a spiritual tradition inaugurated by Zoroaster in Babylon, the tradition of the Magi.

At the culmination of this tradition appeared the three Magi, the three Kings who journeyed from Babylonia to Bethlehem to pay homage to the newborn child. What stands behind this? Here we touch upon one of the deeper mysteries, the significance of which is that the ancient star wisdom had to pass through the 'needle's eye' of Christianity. The three Magi hold the key to this step because as representatives of the ancient star wisdom they came to visit the founder of Christianity. If we are concerned with finding a Christian wisdom of the stars, we must make a connection with the spiritual tradition of the Magi. This means coming to terms with the sidereal zodiac, which was used by the Babylonian priesthood up until about the year AD 75. Around this time Babylonian culture disappeared altogether. Its mission, bound up with the spiritual stream of the Magi, had been completed. With the disappearance of Babylonian culture, the sidereal zodiac vanished from the West. However, it was transmitted to India, where it is still used today, although in a modified form. In the West it disappeared completely and only re-emerged again at the end of the nineteenth century. This came about through the excavation of cuneiform texts from Babylon. The translation of these texts revealed that the Babylonians had used another zodiac, the sidereal zodiac. The ancient sidereal zodiac is different from the tropical zodiac used in present-day astrology, which was introduced by the Greeks. In seeking a Christian star wisdom, we have to return to the original zodiac based on spiritual perception of the reality of the spiritual beings of the cosmos.

It was not coincidence that the sidereal zodiac was rediscovered around the start of the new Michael Age in 1879. For on this basis a new wisdom of the stars can arise, as I have outlined in my *Hermetic Astrology* trilogy, especially in the volume *Christian Hermetic Astrology*, which is concerned with the Star of the Magi and the life of Christ. We need to look at the spiritual tradition of the Magi inaugurated by Zoroaster. Zoroaster taught that he would come again, that he would reincarnate. To his pupils in Babylon he said "I will come again"—impressing upon them that they should watch the stars and read the signs in the heavens until they should see the sign indicating his rebirth. They should then come bearing gifts, to pay homage, because through this rebirth—so he taught—there would appear the Messiah, the Saviour of humanity, who would come, pass through death and descend to the center of the Earth, then rise up to heaven again, later to return with his celestial armies of light. Zoroaster actually described to his pupils a prophetic vision of the future coming of Christ, indicating how he himself would reincarnate to prepare the way for this coming of the Messiah, and emphasizing how important it would be that this be recognized. And it was recognized by three people, the three Magi, but it needed the preparation of the spiritual tradition in order for them to come to this recognition.

The three kings ('magi') were reincarnated pupils of Zoroaster. If we raise the question who they were, we have to look at his pupils, those who came into connection with him. We know that Pythagoras was a pupil of Zoroaster. We know also that Pythagoras travelled extensively. He was born on the island of Samos and travelled to Egypt, where he was initiated into the Egyptian mysteries. He then went to Babylon and was there initiated by Zoroaster. As Porphyry describes in his biography of Pythagoras, "He attached himself to Zaratas (= Zoroaster), by whom he was purified from the pollutions of his past life." Then Pythagoras returned to Greece. There the impulse of Zoroaster, the impulse of cosmic science, was taught in Greece, and then later in Italy through the founding by Pythagoras of a Mystery School at Crotona in Southern Italy. He was one of the reincarnated kings, the one who bore gold to the new-born Jesus.

I mentioned earlier that Zoroaster was related to King Cyrus the Great, who also stood in the service of the Christ impulse. Through Cyrus, who conquered Babylon, the Jewish people were set free from the Babylonian captivity and were able to return to Jerusalem. He gave the command they should return to Jerusalem and rebuild the Temple, which had been destroyed by Nebuchadnezzar II. We know through the excavation of the 'Cyrus cylinder', which has been translated, that Cyrus gave the command for the release of the people of Israel from Babylon, so that they could rebuild the Temple. The rebuilding of the Temple was a sign of active preparation for the approaching incarnation of Christ. The building of the Temple symbolically signified the building of the physical vessel into which Christ would come. The life of Christ would be unthinkable without the Temple in Jerusalem, where he often taught during his ministry. Cyrus the Great also reincarnated as one of the three kings, the king who bore frankincense. Pythagoras bore the gold, gold being the symbol of the wisdom of intelligence, radiant wisdom, which was his special faculty. The special gift of Cyrus was his quality of heart, his great piety. He recognized the spiritual traditions of other peoples, those whom he conquered, and allowed them to carry on their spiritual practices. This quality comes to expression in the gift of the incense, the burning of incense symbolizing religious devotion and piety. This was the quality that King Cyrus brought as his gift.

Who was the third king? We find among the prophets of Israel in captivity in Babylon the prophet Daniel. If we read the Book of Daniel attentively, it is clear that he was singled out among the people of Israel because of his strength of will, and also because of his ability to prophesy, to read the signs of the future. In the esoteric tradition Daniel was referred to as the Man of Will. Further, the name he was given in Babylon is closely related to the name he later received in the Christian tradition. He was named Belteshazzar by the Babylonians. As the third of the Magi, who reincarnated as the king who bore the gift of myrrh, he was named Balthasar. Myrrh signifies the atonement of the will. It is very moving to read the Book of Daniel, to read how Daniel prayed for the people of Israel on account of their sins, praying for their atonement. This quality of will and atonement of the will is signified by the myrrh borne by

the third king. In his life as Daniel, he came into contact with Zoroaster in Babylon, although he was not a pupil of Zoroaster in the
same sense as Pythagoras, who was initiated by Zoroaster. When
Zoroaster reincarnated, he was awaited by his three reincarnated
pupils, who recognized the signs in the stars and then came to pay
homage to him.

We find the background to all of this in Babylonian astrology and
astronomy. Already the German astronomer Kepler tried to identify
what the Star of the Magi was. What was it that the Magi saw in the
heavens? He came to the conclusion that the Star of the Magi was
connected with the threefold conjunction between the planets Jupiter and Saturn in the constellation of Pisces in the year 7 BC. These
two planets met three times during the course of the year 7 BC.
Kepler computed that they were joined by the planet Mars, so that
the three planets Mars, Jupiter, and Saturn were very close together
in the month of March, 6 BC, which is the date he arrived at for the
birth of Jesus. If one follows this up, one can even identify the day,
or rather the evening, of his birth. It was the evening of the Full
Moon in Virgo, which took place on the evening of March 5 in the
year 6 BC The Full Moon in the middle of the Virgin was the sign of
the birth. On that evening the three Magi were gazing up to the
heavens and saw the shining orb of the Full Moon in the Virgin. On
one side of the Virgin they saw her holding the bread, symbolized
by the ear of corn, and on the other side the grapes, symbolizing the
wine. They beheld the disc of the Moon and saw the soul of the
reincarnating Zoroaster descending toward them, coming down to
the Earth. It was this great vision that led them to know that on this
night Jesus was born on Earth. And they also knew from tradition
that Cyrus the Great had freed the people of Israel in order that they
could go back and rebuild the Temple in Jerusalem.

The three kings believed that Zoroaster must have been reborn in
Jerusalem. So they set off to seek the newborn king there. As we
know, they made the mistake of going to King Herod and asking him
the whereabouts of the newborn king. This led to the Massacre of the
Innocents. Remarkably, a tablet has been excavated from Babylon
showing that the Babylonian priesthood had actually computed this
particular day, March 5 in the year 6 BC. On that very day there was a

conjunction between Mars and Jupiter. In fact, they had computed in advance this meeting of Mars and Jupiter on March 5, 6 BC. This was the computational side of what the Magi experienced on an inner plane of vision through spiritual beholding of the starry heavens.

We see therefore that in the sixth century BC, Zoroaster founded the spiritual tradition of the Magi. We now know something about this long-lost tradition and what the point of it was. By way of analogy, just as at that time Zoroaster inaugurated the tradition to prepare for the coming of Christ on the physical plane, so now the task of a new star wisdom is to prepare the way for knowledge and perception of the event of Christ's Second Coming, this time not on the physical plane but in the etheric aura of the Earth. The task of a new wisdom of the stars is connected with deepening our understanding of this event of the Second Coming. And just as Zoroaster defined the zodiac at the time he inaugurated the tradition preparing for the coming of Christ, so this new Christian wisdom of the stars has the task of coming to a new knowledge of the zodiac, and an understanding of what the configurations of the stars in the various constellations of the zodiac mean. This is an important step in coming to a knowledge of what the zodiac is.

The diagram of the sidereal zodiac from Volume I of *Hermetic Astrology* (see Figure 2) shows the dates of entry of the Sun into the signs of the sidereal zodiac as they are at the present time. On the other hand there is the division known as the tropical zodiac, which most people are familiar with. We need to come to an understanding of the relationship between these two zodiacs, and what the significance of each of them is. A fundamental scientific principle is not to accept something purely on faith. A scientist will always test and research the matter at hand. He will not blindly accept it on faith, because this can lead to superstition. Here we come to the kernel of a problem relevant to the whole of modern astrology. As long as one does not understand the whole background of what one is working with—in this case the zodiac, which as everybody knows is fundamental to both astronomy and astrology—one cannot really understand what the zodiac is. One is just accepting something as a matter of faith, which amounts to superstition. Therefore, looking at the question of what the zodiac is, in the first place it is a matter of trying to penetrate to an understanding of something. This question has different levels. There is the spiritual level, relating to the spiritual beings working through the signs of the zodiac, and there is the more scientific level. I would like to illustrate this by considering the significance of the zodiac for our daily life.

Figure 2

The Sidereal Zodiac

Reproduced from *Hermetic Astrology*, vol. I, p 9,
with the dates of the Sun's entrance into the Signs
(e.g., the Sun enters the sidereal sign of Aries on April 15)

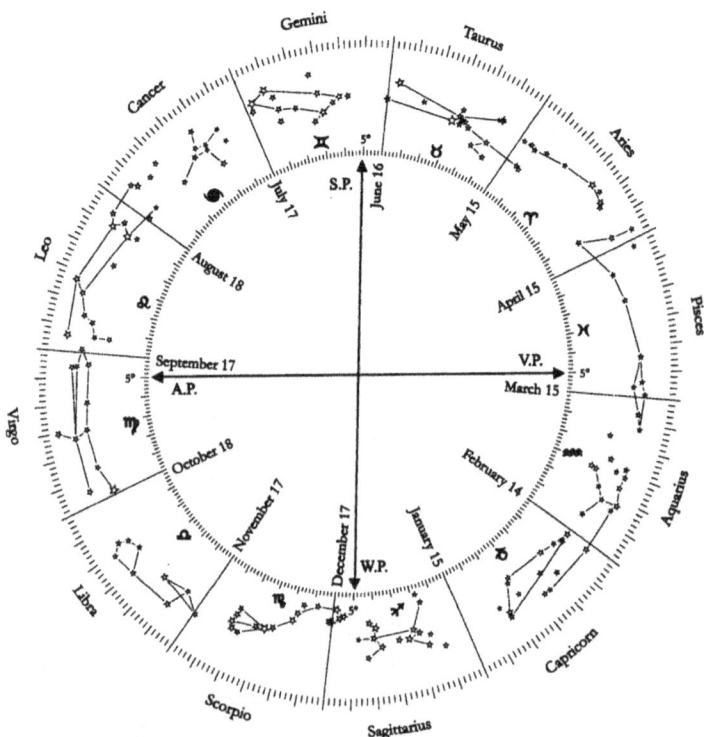

V.P. (vernal point) = location of Sun on (or around) March 21
S.P. (summer solstice) = location of Sun on (or around) June 22
A.P. (autumnal point) = location of Sun on (or around) September 23
W.P. (winter solstice) = location of Sun on (or around) December 22

Some of you will recall what I said regarding the approaching Full Moon. Last night the Moon was at the tail end of the Scorpion and this morning it passed into Sagittarius. Tomorrow evening, if it is clear, we shall be able to see the Full Moon in Sagittarius. The actual moment of the Full Moon is around 5 o'clock tomorrow afternoon, when the Moon will be Full in the middle of sidereal Sagittarius, at 17 degrees Sagittarius. This means that the Sun is opposite in the zodiac at the time of Full Moon, since by definition at the Full Moon the Sun and the Moon are opposite one another in the zodiac. At the time of the Full Moon, therefore, the Sun will be in the middle of Gemini, at 17 degrees Gemini. This corresponds with what can be perceived in relation to the sidereal zodiac, since the Sun enters sidereal Gemini on June 16 and remains there until July 17. Thus today, July 2, the Sun is exactly in the middle of Gemini. For some this may seem to contradict everything known up until now about the zodiac. It might indeed seem very strange. Nevertheless, everything would become clear if an eclipse of the Sun were to take place. Normally we cannot see where the Sun is because it is too bright; we are unable to see the zodiacal background of the Sun. But if at this moment an eclipse of the Sun were to take place, we could go out and look up and see the Sun against the background of the stars of Gemini, in spite of the fact that most astrologers here in the West say that the Sun is in Cancer. How are we to understand this?

The conception of the zodiac held by most modern Western astrologers is that of the tropical zodiac. The tropical zodiac was introduced into astrology by Claudius Ptolemy around the middle of the second century AD. When Ptolemy introduced the tropical zodiac there was no problematic difference of the kind just mentioned, because the tropical zodiac at that time more or less coincided with the sidereal zodiac. The basis of the tropical zodiac is that it starts with the vernal point—the location of the Sun in the zodiac on March 21. At the time of Ptolemy the vernal point was at 1 degree Aries in the sidereal zodiac. This was about AD 150. But the vernal point moves. It moves backward through the zodiac at a rate of one degree in 72 years, so the vernal point was at 0 degrees Aries around AD 220. This is the time when the two zodiacs coincided. Thus it did not make any difference for Ptolemy or for people living shortly after him which zodiac they used. They were the same. But since that time the vernal point has shifted from the start of Aries back through Pisces and is now at 5 degrees Pisces. Obviously it makes a big difference whether one measures the zodiac from the vernal point (tropical zodiac) or takes the actual constellations of the zodiac (sidereal zodiac). The problem is that with the collapse and disappearance of Babylonian culture, the sidereal zodiac vanished and the tropical zodiac was substituted in its place, at least in the West. In the East, in India, the sidereal zodiac is still used, although Indian astrologers define the zodiac in a way that differs slightly from that of the original Babylonian zodiac. But to all intents and purposes the Indian zodiac is identical to the Babylonian sidereal zodiac.

Most Western astrologers use the following argument to justify the validity of the tropical zodiac. They say, "Of course it is the tropical zodiac that is valid! Look at how the seasons relate to this zodiac. We find that in the time of Aries after March 21 the plants begin to sprout and grow, then in Virgo everything ripens, and in Scorpio everything dies and fades away—you see there is a perfect harmony between the growth of nature and the tropical zodiac." This is an argument commonly used by tropical astrologers. But it has a fatal flaw. It works only for the northern hemisphere. For people in Australia the time following March 21 is not when plants start to grow. It is the time when everything starts to fade away. So what is the tropical zodiac?

This is easy to establish on the basis of historical research. Originally it was not a zodiac at all, but a solar calendar. It was defined in Athens by the Greek astronomer Euctemon in the fifth century BC. He said, "Let us count the number of days from the vernal equinox. First we count 31 days and we call this the month of Aries; then we count the next 31 days and this we call the month of Taurus. The third month thus counted off we call the month of Gemini. . . ." The end of the third month coincides with the summer solstice. Here there began a count of 30 days for the month of Cancer. And so on. In this way the year was divided into twelve solar months related to the vernal equinox, summer solstice, autumnal equinox, and winter solstice. This was a very practical calendar (see Figure 3). But what

confuses things is that the months were named after the signs of the
sidereal zodiac. So the first month is named after the sign of Aries,
and the subsequent months were named correspondingly.

Figure 3

Euctemon's Solar Calendar, with Twelve Solar Months

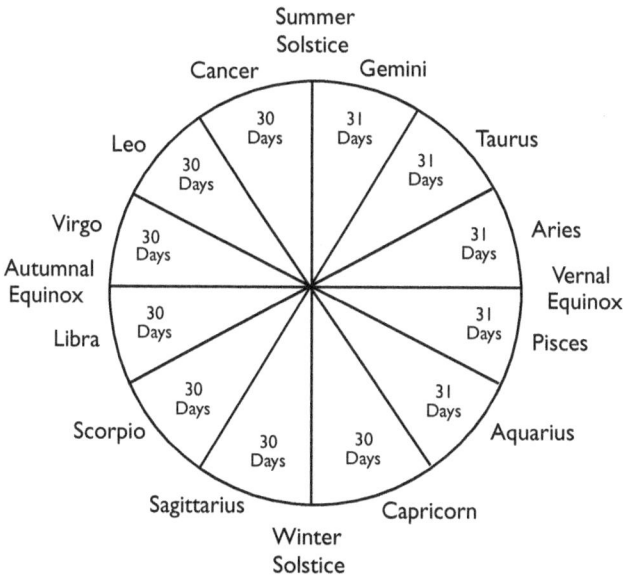

The people of antiquity thought in terms of correspondences.
The Greeks thought there must be a correspondence between the
cycle of the year divided into twelve months and the twelve signs of
the stellar zodiac. So they established this correspondence simply by
saying that, as the cycle of the year begins with the first month, the
month following the vernal equinox, this month is the month of
Aries because it corresponds to the first sign in the cycle of the twelve
signs in the heavens. The same holds true with regard to the remaining months of the solar calendar, which was the forerunner of the
tropical zodiac. So we find there is indeed a reality to the tropical
zodiac. But the reality is that it is a *calendar* and not a zodiac. The

word zodiac means the circle of living creatures, and this relates to the sublime spiritual beings who radiate down from the twelve cosmic signs embedded in the zodiacal constellations of the fixed stars.

The tropical zodiac, then, is not a zodiac—it is a calendar. For example, anyone born in the northern hemisphere on March 25 is born in the month of Aries. But on this date the Sun stands in the sign of Pisces in the sidereal zodiac. In other words, the tropical calendar relates to the cycle of nature in the course of the year. It relates solely to the Sun's movement up and down, its movement in declination. At the time of the spring equinox on March 21, day and night are equal in length and the Sun rises due East and sets due West. After March 21 the Sun rises higher and higher. This is known in astronomy as the movement of the Sun in declination. It has nothing to do with the location of the Sun against the background of the zodiac. It has to do solely with its movement in declination. The Sun attains maximum northerly declination around June 22, the day of the summer solstice. So what takes place here? Because the Sun is ascending, its light and warmth are increasing and the nature spirits (the so-called elemental beings) are drawn out and up by the increasing light and warmth of the Sun, which breathes through the whole of nature. This is what accounts for the growth of plants during this time of the year. What we call spring is the time of the rising up of the elemental spirits attracted by the rising of the Sun, and this accounts for growth in nature. The Sun reaches its high point at the summer solstice. After this day, which is the longest day (the shortest night), the Sun begins to descend in declination again, continuing in this way till the fall equinox. During this time of descent nature expands. Everything ripens and blossoms. After the fall equinox the Sun descends below the celestial equator and begins its movement in southerly declination. When it attains maximum southerly declination at the winter solstice, the Sun is at its deepest point. With this downward movement of the Sun after the fall equinox the elemental spirits withdraw into the Earth. It is a time of decay, when there is no more growth. Around the deepest point is a time of hibernation. It is here that the winter solstice takes place. Following the winter solstice, the Sun begins to rise again and the gradual releasing of the elemental spirits from the Earth begins.

The tropical calendar describes the cycle of growth and decay in nature. It relates to the activity of the nature spirits. The correspondence with the signs of the zodiac is actually very appropriate, for we can say that the sign of Aries in the heavens is the first sign when something new begins. In the solar calendar the month of Aries is likewise the time when the new cycle of nature begins. The correspondence is very profound. In other words Euctemon, who devised this solar calendar, did so out of a profound intuition. However, if the tropical calendar is applied in the southern hemisphere (some of you may have lived down under and experienced there the reversal of the seasons), the solar calendar has to be reversed, so that what we call the month of Aries here between March 21 and April 20 is in the southern hemisphere—as far as the nature spirits are concerned—the month of Libra. Or what we call here the month of Cancer, when the Sun is at its highest, down under is the month of Capricorn. Someone born today [July 2] in the northern hemisphere is born in the month of Cancer in terms of the solar calendar underlying the tropical zodiac. On the other hand, if born in the southern hemisphere, he or she would be born there in the month of Capricorn. Yet both are born with the Sun in the middle of Gemini, for the Sun is now close to the middle of sidereal Gemini. This is the same all around the world, and this is the important thing from an astrological point of view, namely, what forces the human being—descending from heavenly realms— bears into Earthly incarnation from the world of the stars.

From an astrological point of view it is quite irrelevant what is happening in the world of nature, just as, for example, were a person to go out into the sunshine when it is very hot and get sunburnt, we would not ascribe this to an astrological effect of the Sun. Similarly, whether one is born in midwinter or midsummer is a secondary phenomenon as compared to the fact that the human soul descends from the world of stars having built up its physical, etheric, and astral bodies out of that world. This is the significant thing.

It is crucial, then, to understand what the tropical zodiac really is. Again, it is not a zodiac. It is not a circle of living beings. It is a *calendar*. And it is important to understand how to apply this calendar, which must be reversed in the southern hemisphere. This knowledge, combined with years of research on the larger historical question of the zodiac, has led me to conclude that the true astrological zodiac is the ancient sidereal zodiac as defined in Babylon in the 6th century BC by the great initiate Zoroaster on the basis of his profound spiritual clairvoyance, which enabled him to specify exactly where the spheres of influence of the holy living creatures underlying the signs of the sidereal zodiac lie.

It is also possible to show through reincarnation research that the sidereal zodiac is the authentic astrological zodiac, according to which the soul orients its reincarnation upon the Earth. Those interested in following this up can look at examples given in Volume I of my book *Hermetic Astrology*. And I would add by way of conclusion that what one finds in the astrological tradition of the West concerning the qualities of the zodiacal signs is not reliable. In this connection it is interesting to read what Greek astrologers have to say, for example, about the sign of Scorpio. If you compare this with what modern astrologers say about Scorpio, you will find that the modern description incorporates elements of the Greek description of both Libra and Scorpio. In other words, the modern description is a mixture of Libra and Scorpio. This means that astrologers have unconsciously picked up on the shift due to the precession of the equinoxes and compensated on a subconscious level to accommodate this shift. Thus what originally was called Scorpio is now a mixture of Scorpio and Libra, which means one cannot simply take the descriptions as they are given in the astrological textbooks but one has to do research. One has to look into the qualities of the zodiacal signs in a new way. Here something of the importance of eurythmy as a means of coming to an understanding of the forces at work in the zodiacal signs will more and more be recognized. One has to take all of this in a spirit of open-mindedness. Nonetheless, many people feel an instinctive antipathy to a new way of looking at the zodiac because they are used to identifying themselves with a particular zodiacal sign. On the other hand, it is good to consider new things and remain open. What is called for is an open-minded consideration of these things, and it can be a help to look at the biographies of historical personalities in trying to arrive at an objective view.

Christ
and the Zodiac

As a starting point, let us consider the idea that the whole of the ancient star wisdom needs to be Christianized. When we look up to the signs of the zodiac we contemplate animal figures—the Ram, the Bull, the Lion, and so on—this is a symbolism that speaks of twelve holy animals. The zodiac is an animal circle (the German word for zodiac is *Tierkreis*, which means 'animal circle'). We can also ask: What is the *Menschenkreis* (the 'human circle') in connection with the signs of the zodiac? In this way we are able to arrive at a Christian understanding of the signs of the zodiac. But before we go further with the theme 'Christ and the Zodiac', let us look briefly at some remaining questions from the preceding chapter.

The first question concerns the Babylonian sidereal zodiac, in which the constellations are divided equally into signs of thirty degrees. This goes back to Zoroaster and his clairvoyant vision. He was able to describe the extent of the spiritual influence of the spiritual beings—the holy living creatures who work through the constellations. He arrived at an arrangement where each constellation is apportioned to one of twelve thirty-degree signs. This contrasts with the unequal divisions of the astronomical zodiac used in modern astronomy, which has a different foundation from the Babylonian sidereal zodiac. The zodiac used in modern astronomy goes back to Claudius Ptolemy (second century BC). Not only did he introduce the tropical zodiac as the basis of modern Western astrology, but he also introduced the unequal-division astronomical zodiac used by modern astronomy. What was originally one—the signs and the constellations having been *one and the same* for the Babylonians—was divided by Ptolemy into the so-called signs (usually understood as the signs of the tropical zodiac) and the constellations, which are understood as being unequal divisions. For example, the modern astronomical constellation of the Virgin extends about halfway into the Babylonian Libra. What actually took place here, with the arising of these unequal divisions? How did this come about?

We have to remember that Ptolemy was an intellectual genius. He knew most of the astronomy of his day. He gathered together everything he could lay his hands on—all the observations extending back centuries earlier—and on this basis was able to draw up the Ptolemaic world system. This was the ancient geocentric system of the universe, in which the Earth is conceived of as being at the center, and described by Ptolemy as consisting of nested concentric spheres formed by the planets around the Earth: first the Moon sphere, then Mercury, Venus, the Sun, and so on. The system Ptolemy worked out is very complicated and ingenious. He was able to describe the movements of the planets to a high degree of accuracy using this astronomical system. This remained the view of the universe down through the centuries until Copernicus published his book on the heliocentric system in 1543. Up until that time everyone believed that the Sun goes round the Earth and that all the planets revolve round the Earth also—and then Copernicus' book was published. However, it took several centuries before the idea that the Earth and the planets revolve around the Sun became widely established. Ptolemy's influence on the history of astronomy was phenomenal. He himself was quite open and honest about how he arrived at the division of the constellations into unequal stellar groupings. On the basis of his physical observations of the stars, he simply catalogued them—following the lead of his predecessor, the Greek astronomer Hipparchus. Ptolemy openly admits changing some of the designations of Hipparchus.

Ptolemy's catalogue of stars, which led to unequal divisions of the constellations, was based primarily on his physical perception of the groupings of the stars. It had nothing to do with clairvoyance. Unlike Zoroaster, who arrived at the original definition of the zodiac as comprising twelve constellations apportioned equally to twelve signs each thirty degrees long—the astronomical zodiac introduced by Ptolemy and still used today is not based on clairvoyance. It is simply a catalogue of the stars based on physical observation. How did this come about?

Let us consider an example. Those who have been to Paris and visited the Louvre Museum will probably have seen the zodiac of Dendera, which Napoleon had transported back to Paris when he conquered Egypt. This is a circular zodiac that was on the ceiling of the Hathor temple at Dendera. There we see the Egyptian gods placed around the zodiac. We clearly see the figure of the Virgin as a standing figure. One hand reaches out toward the tail of the Lion; the other holds the ear of corn marked by the star Spica. She is standing. Yet Ptolemy shows the Virgin as lying down (and this has been universally adopted in modern star maps). This makes her much longer, her feet extending halfway into Libra. What does this signify? We may think of the Virgin as representing an aspect of the Divine Sophia, the divine wisdom. The fact that her posture is changed from standing to lying symbolizes the loss of the divine wisdom. Sophia has been lost from view. To find the Divine Sophia again would signify symbolically raising her to her rightful standing position.

Another consequence of Ptolemy's redefining of the zodiac becomes evident from Egyptian depictions of the zodiac. In these the figure of Sophia as the figure of Isis, the standing Virgin, is shown with a figure to her right holding the scales. This is the balance-holder holding the scales. Who is this in Christian iconography? It is the Archangel Michael holding the scales. As a consequence of what Ptolemy did in taking the Virgin from a standing to a lying position, with her feet extending halfway into Libra almost up to the scales, Michael disappeared altogether from the zodiac. Michael, who is really the Guardian of the Threshold holding the balance between the upper and the lower worlds, has been displaced from the zodiac through the loss of the ancient clairvoyance. Again, it is a task for a new imaginative perception of the zodiac to recover the representation of Sophia as the Virgin and also of Michael as Protector of the divine wisdom, as the figure who holds the scales for the judgement of souls in the life after death. All this came about because of Ptolemy's intellectual speculations, bereft of clairvoyance. The living visions of the signs were lost. We must find them again. It is our task to overcome this intellectual construction of the modern astronomical zodiac with its unequal divisions, to find again the true signs as they shine out to us through the equal divisions of the sidereal zodiac.

The other question remaining from our last discussion is that of interpretation; that is, if we change from the tropical to the sidereal zodiac, how do we make the switch in interpretation? Let us take as an example the German poet and playwright Goethe, who is most famous for his drama *Faust*. He was born on August 28. For modern Western astrologers this means he was born in the sign of Virgo. But we have seen that this really signifies that he was born in the month of Virgo in the *solar calendar*, and on August 28 the Sun is actually in the middle of the constellation of Leo. There is however a quite natural tendency, if we believe something in advance, to see only what we already believe. In other words, astrologers who believe Goethe is a Virgo see him through the perspective of Virgo. This is how they conceive him, and when they read his biography they see only what corresponds to this conception: such things as that he was in the service of Count Carl August of Weimar, that he made many observations, wrote much, and so on. Yet if one considers him as a Leo, one suddenly gets a totally different perspective of Goethe. One sees him as the king of the poets, as the center of a wide cultural circle in Germany, as a man of tremendous heart warmth, a lion of a personality. Here we see how our *a priori* conceptions color the way we see the world. Of course it is a question of overcoming this subjective element, of trying to find an objective means of discovering the truth. This is really a lifetime's task.

One way to begin is to study biographies. For example, looking at those born in sidereal Aries (connected with the head) we find that many of the great thinkers and philosophers were born when the Sun was in sidereal Aries, and also many of those with claims to being leaders—for example Charlemagne, Oliver Cromwell, Robespierre, Lenin, Hitler (who called himself *Führer*, 'leader'), and Isabella of Castile and Catherine the Great, two of the most formidable queens of history. Thinkers born in sidereal Aries include Immanuel Kant, Karl Marx, and Sigmund Freud, each of whom constructed influential philosophical systems, in the later two cases captivating millions of people. Also some of the great leaders from the realm of the arts, such as Leonardo da Vinci, William Shakespeare, the German Romantic poet Novalis, and the composers Brahms and Tchaikovsky, were born under sidereal Aries.

On the other hand, what do we find in the case of those born in sidereal Pisces, which Rudolf Steiner describes as a sign of creativity, seeing that Pisces is connected with the feet and also with the hands through which we create? Many great creative artists were born when the Sun was in sidereal Pisces: the painters Raphael, Michelangelo, and Van Gogh, the German poets Hölderlin, Hebbel, and Hamerling, the composers Bach, Haydn, and Rachmaninov, are only a few examples of creative artists born in sidereal Pisces.

Of course, everything depends on how one goes about doing such research. Hopefully in the course of time, if sufficient people are able to contribute to research in this area, it will prove possible to establish a more objective view of the twelve signs of the zodiac than that handed down to us by an astrological tradition based largely upon conceptions with no basis in reality. We all know something about these kinds of conceptions, which are often based on simple association—for example the conception of Taurus: 'He behaves like a bull in a china shop,' and so on. Very often the sort of argumentation brought in favor of the tropical zodiac is purely subjective. One leading astrologer in Germany told me she knew the tropical zodiac was the true zodiac because her two grandchildren, born under Leo, both 'roared like lions.' Such an interpretation has no scientific validity whatsoever.

We are confronted with a huge task: to throw out erroneous conceptions and to do solid research in order to arrive at true conceptions of the qualities of the zodiacal signs. Here we stand at the beginning of a new star wisdom. This is a work that requires cooperation between many people. Fortunately there are helpful indications—for example, from anthroposophy, eurythmy, and through looking into the life of Christ. All of this, taken together, comprises a path that can open up a new star wisdom rising beyond the level of personality to a completely new level, to a spiritual understanding of the zodiac.

Returning now to the theme of this chapter, that of Christ and the zodiac, what can we say? This afternoon we looked at the precession of the equinoxes, the retrograde movement of the vernal point through the signs of the sidereal zodiac. There is also another very interesting point: this movement, which is a movement of 1 degree in 72 years, corresponds to the average length of a human being's life on Earth. Here a cosmic background to our human existence on Earth becomes apparent. Taking the equal division of the sidereal zodiac into signs of 30 degrees each, the vernal point takes 2,160 years to move retrograde through one sign (30 x 72 = 2,160). This movement gives rise to the astrological ages. Because the vernal point is currently at 5 degrees Pisces, we say that at the present time we are living in the Age of Pisces. Every astrologer in the world, whether a sidereal astrologer in India or a tropical astrologer in the West, agrees that the position of the vernal point in the sidereal zodiac is an astrological reality. But they do not all agree as to where the vernal point is. Some believe the vernal point has already entered Aquarius: again this is usually on the basis of purely subjective thinking and erroneous conceptions, without looking at the actual facts. For example, one justification often presented in favour of the argument that the vernal point is now in Aquarius is that Aquarius is an air sign and that in the twentieth century aviation developed. The underlying thought is that since humanity has entered into the air we are in the Age of Aquarius. However, every astronomical map shows the vernal point beneath the Western Fish in the constellation of Pisces, the exact location being 5 degrees Pisces.

Now we come to an interesting question. Let us suppose that every astrologer would also agree that the vernal point is currently at 5 degrees Pisces, and would agree that this is a spiritual reality. If it is a spiritual reality that the vernal point is here in Pisces, why not—it's just a short step—say it is also a spiritual reality if the planet Saturn is in Pisces, or the Sun, or any other planet. In other words, if, for example, the planet Saturn is in conjunction with the vernal point, and the vernal point is located at 5 degrees Pisces, it follows that Saturn is also at 5 degrees Pisces, especially as in astrology a conjunction means *working together*. It's a kind of 'double think' to say that Saturn is at 0 degrees Aries and the vernal point is at 5 degrees Pisces and that they are nevertheless in conjunction. This is one example of the kind of anomaly in astrology that tropical astrologers have not come to terms with. Generally speaking, this way of thinking is inconsistent and does not take account of the astronomical realities.

What arises from this movement of the vernal point through the sidereal signs? The astrological ages are each 2,160 years in length. Through determining the location of the vernal point, we are able to arrive at an exact dating of the astrological ages. For example, when the vernal point has moved through these remaining 5 degrees, it will enter Aquarius and the Age of Aquarius will begin. The Age of Aquarius will start in the year 2375. The Age of Pisces started about the year AD 220. The interval from 220 to 2375 is not exactly 2,160 years. It would be if the starting date were AD 215. But the vernal point does not move precisely 1 degree every 72 years. This is its average rate of motion around the zodiac, but at present the vernal point is moving slightly faster than this, which is why the 'average date' for the start of the Age of Pisces would be AD 215, although the actual astronomical date was in the year AD 220. If we look at this movement around the whole circle of the zodiac, it would take 12 x 2,160 years to pass through the twelve signs, and this would be 25,920 years. This is the great Platonic year. We find many interesting correspondences connected with this. For example, it is the average number of days a human being lives on Earth, if he lives for roughly 71 years. It is also the number of breaths a human being takes on average in one day. We find this number over and over again.

Coming back to the realm of music, let us consider again the question of the keys. The whole tone system depends upon how the notes are tuned. An orchestra tunes to the note A, but the frequency to which A is tuned varies in different orchestras. The composer and conductor Verdi decreed at the State Opera in Milan in 1882 that A should be 432 vibrations per second. But in Vienna today it is for example much higher, at least 442 or even 444. This is symptomatic of the time in which we live, where everything is speeding up. Nevertheless A = 432 is really the cosmic frequency, as indicated also by Rudolf Steiner. What is interesting about this is that if this is the number of vibrations in a second to produce the note A, what do we have in one minute? We have again 25,920 (= 60 x 432). If one works in eurythmy with these different tunings, one finds that if one moves to this single note A tuned at 432, it works in a harmonious way upon the whole organism, from the head down to the feet, whereas if one tries to move to A = 442, which is the usual frequency nowadays, this works more upon the head. The tendency to tune to an ever-higher frequency is a sign that we are increasingly losing touch with the realities of the heart. Instead, only the excitement of the higher-pitched note is sought. All tampering with tuning the system of keys throws the whole system out of its cosmic alignment. I mention this as an aside to show that there is a profound cosmic background to the sounds of music.

Let us now look more closely at the precession of the equinoxes. Everyone familiar with anthroposophy will know that Rudolf Steiner referred to the movement of the vernal point through the constellations as giving rise to historical periods which he called cultural epochs. For example, he describes the Egypto-Babylonian Age as connected with Taurus, the Greco-Roman Age as connected with Aries, and our present European Age—European culture that since the time of the Renaissance has spread out across the whole world—as connected with Pisces. The cultural epochs are a manifestation on the cultural level of the precession of the equinoxes on a spiritual level. Rudolf Steiner gave exact dates for the cultural epochs on the basis of his clairvoyant research. He pointed out that the cultural epochs are each 2,160 years in length. We need only take account of this fact to grasp the spiritual reality underlying the twelve zodiacal constellations, namely, that they must be equal length, for otherwise the cultural epochs would be unequal in length. This is readily understandable to everyone. However, it is rather more complicated to explain how the dates Rudolf Steiner gave for the cultural epochs in fact correspond exactly with the precession of the vernal point through the Babylonian sidereal zodiac, thereby showing that this is the true zodiac. Anyone interested in following this up will find a detailed description of the dating of the cultural epochs in connection with the precession of the equinoxes in chapter 3 of my book *Hermetic Astrology*, Volume I.

Those familiar with anthroposophy will also know that Rudolf Steiner described how through the different cultural ages the being of Christ in each age formed a new and different relationship with humanity. So, in looking at Christ in relationship to the zodiac, the astrological ages are of great significance. Let us start with the Age of Cancer. For this we must go back to about 8000 BC, to the time of the most ancient civilization as determined by archaeological excavations. Nothing much older than 8000 BC has been found up until now. The archaeological excavation of Jericho, for example, leads back to about 8000 BC as the date for the oldest remains. This was the time of the first culture after the destruction of Atlantis. The center of this ancient culture in the Age of Cancer was India. There the people of India related to the being of Christ under the name of *Vishvakarma*, whom they saw as a majestic being embracing the whole world of the stars.

Following the precession of the equinoxes further, we come to the Age of Gemini, which takes us back to about 6000 BC. The center of cultural development at that time was in Persia. There the ancient Persian prophet Zarathustra taught of humanity's relationship to Christ, whom he called *Ahura Mazdao*, the aura of the Sun. Also, they referred to Christ's evil twin, *Ahriman*, the dark spirit connected with the Earth, who was the opponent of Christ. The ancient Persian religion describes the war or battle between Christ and Ahriman. Ahriman, the evil twin, challenges Ahura Mazdao, and says, "I will win over all your followers, all those human beings who belong to you; I will win them over in the course of time to become my followers." And Ahura Mazdao's response is to accept the challenge by laying down a set period of time in which this battle for the souls of human beings is to take place. If we follow this dating, it emerges that we are now in the historical period of time when this struggle is approaching a culmination. We could say that behind everything that has taken place in the world is the battle between Ahura Mazdao (Christ) and Ahriman for the possession of the human soul. This is the background to our present world situation.

Following the precession of the equinoxes further, we come, after the Age of Gemini, to the Age of Taurus, when the Egyptian and Babylonian cultures reached their high point. The pyramids are characteristic for the Egypto-Babylonian culture. They are very Taurean-like constructions with their powerful bases upon the Earth and their points reaching up to the heavens. Just as the bull has its horns which reach up to the heavens as spiritual antennae, so the pyramids reach up to the heavens acting as spiritual antennae to receive forces and revelations from the spiritual world. In the Age of Taurus, Christ was worshipped as Osiris in Egypt. In the early stages of Egyptian culture *Osiris* was seen in connection with the Sun, and then later in connection with the Moon. We find through the Ages a gradual descent of Christ from the realm of Stars in ancient India in the Age of Cancer, to the Sun in the Age of Gemini in ancient Persia, and then in the course of the Egyptian civilization, to the Moon. There is a wonderful ancient Egyptian myth concerning Osiris and his consort *Isis*, related to the phases of the Moon. This myth was taught by the priests of Hermes. Here the opponent of Osiris (Christ) is described not as Ahriman but as *Seth* (or *Set*). According to this myth Seth tries to overwhelm Osiris and in the end succeeds in murdering him. Seth sees to it that parts of Osiris' corpse are scattered throughout Egypt. However, Isis seeks the different parts of Osiris and re-members him through fourteen stages. This is connected to the phases of the Moon, the building up of Osiris taking place in fourteen stages or phases from the New Moon to the Full Moon. At the Full Moon, Osiris appears in all his splendor. Then from the Full Moon to the New Moon he is again dismembered through fourteen phases. This is a cosmic myth relating to the phases of the Moon.

The last stage of Christ's descent took place in the Age of Aries, the Greco-Roman period. Having come down from the Stars, to the Sun, to the Moon, in the Age of Aries the incarnation of Christ—his birth upon the Earth—occurred. This had been prepared for by the tradition of the Magi, inaugurated by Zoroaster. It was of course also prepared for by the people of Israel. In the Age of Aries the incarnation of Christ on the Earth took place, and John the Baptist heralded him with the words, "Behold the Lamb of God who bears the sins of the world." The Lamb relates to Aries, the sign of the Ram, who was sacrificed for humanity. Thus, there was a new revelation of Christ in the Age of Aries.

At the same time, in his life's teaching and work Christ prepared the way for the approaching Age of Pisces. During the life of Christ the vernal point was at 2½ degrees Aries; it was right at the beginning of Aries and about to pass over into Pisces. It is significant in this connection that Christ gathered his disciples from among fishermen. And there are further indications that point to the coming Age of Pisces. For example, at the start of the Age of Pisces, around the year AD 220, in the catacombs the symbol of Christ ✳ was used, a symbol that also means fish. Here Christ is designated as the fish. IXΘΥΣ—*Ichthys* (*I-Ch-Th-Y-S*). Ichthys, a Greek word meaning fish, was understood to mean Ich for *Ie*ßoūs *Ch*ristòs (Jesus Christ), then Th Y for *Th*eoū (h) *Y*iòs (God's son) and S for *S*otér (Saviour). "Ιησους Χριστὸς Θεου Υιὸς Σωτηρ—Jesus Christ, God's Son, Saviour," this was the word Ichthys (fish). In the Walking on the Water we see a manifestation of Christ in the power of the Divine Fish. And now a further question arises as to the next manifestation of Christ for the approaching Age of Aquarius.

Before considering this question further, let us dwell upon an important aspect of the new wisdom of the stars—that the Magi were prepared through their star knowledge for the coming birth of Jesus. As discussed in my book *Chronicle of the Living Christ*,[1] Jesus was born on the evening of March 5 in the year 6 BC. It was the night of the Full Moon in Virgo. Where was the Sun in the zodiac at this birth of Jesus as described in the Gospel of Matthew, the Jesus visited by the three Magi? It was in Pisces. The Full Moon was more or less in the middle of Virgo, the Sun opposite in Pisces. Here we see this incarnation of Jesus, reported in the Gospel of Matthew, in the sign of Pisces. However, considering the life of Christ, which fell in the last part of the Age of Aries, we find the overwhelming significance of the sign of Aries.

Just to mention a few examples: the Transfiguration on Mt. Tabor took place at around midnight April 3/4 in the year AD 31, and the Sun that night was at 14 degrees Aries—more or less in the middle of Aries. This was exactly two years prior to the Crucifixion on Golgotha, when the Sun was again in the middle of Aries. This means that all the events connected with the Passion, beginning with the Last Supper on the evening of Thursday April 2 in the year AD 33, the trial by Pontius Pilate, the Scourging, the Carrying of the Cross, and

1. *Chronicle of the Living Christ: The Life and Ministry of Jesus Christ, Foundations of Cosmic Christianity* (Hudson, NY: Anthroposophic Press, 1996).

all the stages of the Passion took place as the Sun was moving from 13 to 14 degrees Aries. Following the Crucifixion there took place the descent of Christ into hell, the descent to the Divine Mother in the underworld, when the Sun was in the 15th degree of Aries. This was followed by the Resurrection on Easter Sunday morning when the Sun was at 15½ degrees Aries. The central impulse of Earth evolution is connected with the Sun in the middle of Aries. Then following on from this, the day after Easter Sunday—on that Monday afternoon—the Risen One appeared to the two disciples, Luke and Cleophas, as they were walking to the town of Emmaus, and there Christ joined them in his resurrection body. When they reached Emmaus, Christ gave them the communion of bread and they recognized who he was. They rushed back to Jerusalem, where the disciples were gathered together in prayer in the Coenaculum, and spoke of what had taken place in Emmaus. Thereupon the Risen One appeared to the ten of them—ten, because neither Judas (having committed suicide on Good Friday) nor Thomas were there. At the end of that week, on Saturday evening, there took place a manifestation of the Risen One to the eleven disciples. This time Thomas was there. Christ said to Thomas, "Put your fingers in my wounds," and it was only then, when Thomas touched him, that he knew this was Christ who had overcome death and was really there in his resurrected form.

All of this transpired as the Sun was in Aries. In the middle of the following week, when Peter, John, and five other disciples were in a fishing boat on the way from Tiberias to the northeast side of the lake of Galilee, they saw a figure on the beach. Again it was the Risen One—this is described in the Gospel of John, where Peter then sprang from the boat and swam to the shore. The conversation between Christ and Peter took place, in which Christ instructed Peter three times with the words, "Feed my sheep," after having asked, "Do you love me?" At this point the Sun was at 25 degrees Aries, still in sidereal Aries. Two days later Christ appeared to the 500 disciples gathered on a mountain in Galilee. Again the Sun was in sidereal Aries. In the case of all the main events connected with the Mystery of Golgotha, and also these appearances of Christ as the Risen One, the Sun was in Aries. He truly was the Lamb of God, the lamb (or ram) being a symbol of the zodiacal sign of Aries.

We can ask, "What about the other signs of the zodiac?" The Ascension of Christ into heaven took place forty days after Easter Sunday, on May 14, in the year A D 33. On that day the Sun was at 23 degrees in sidereal Taurus. This quality of the Ascension—Christ ascending to heaven, that is, leaving the physical plane, and at the same time giving the impulse for the raising up of the whole of existence to the kingdom of the Father—is connected with the impulse of Taurus. Then, ten days later, came the Whitsun event, the descent of the Holy Spirit upon the disciples gathered in the Coenaculum around the Blessed Virgin Mary, when the incarnation of Sophia into Mary took place, an event closely bound up with the descent of the Holy Spirit.[2] This tremendous impulse of communion between the physical world and the spiritual world—an extraordinary event which led that day to the baptizing of three thousand people at the pool of Bethesda—signified the founding of the Church. This event took place as the Sun was in Gemini. We have here very powerful and wonderful imaginations for the zodiacal signs in connection with the life of Christ: the Mystery of Golgotha, the Death and Resurrection, the manifestations of the Risen One— all connected with Aries; the Ascension to heaven, connected with Taurus; Whitsun, the descent of the Holy Spirit—this tremendous community impulse—connected with Gemini.

If one looks for major events in the life of Christ in connection with Cancer, one scarcely finds anything. But there is another very important event connected with Cancer, and this is the birth of the being described in the Gospel of Luke as Mary—Mary of Nazareth—who was born in the night July 17/18 in the year 17 BC, when the Sun was at 25 degrees in sidereal Cancer. Here we have a wonderful image of Cancer, which is the sign very often connected with the motherly quality, the treasuring of all that is the warmth of the home. We may think of the crab that carries its home on its back. Using this symbolism we can feel something of the deep inner quality connected with the innocent being of Mary of Nazareth, who was born when the Sun was in Cancer.

2. See Valentin Tomberg, *Christ and Sophia* (Gt. Barrington, MA: SteinerBooks, 2007), New Testament Meditation Twelve.

Coming now to Leo, there was a most powerful event in the life of Christ when the Sun was in Leo. It was the greatest of his miracles. This was the raising of Lazarus from the dead, which took place when the Sun and Moon were in conjunction with the star Regulus, the heart of the Lion. With this event we can feel the strength of the spirit force of Leo in the overcoming of death, for the risen Lazarus took up a special mission, a special task, to bear the heart of the Christ Impulse connected with the Sun in Leo.

Looking now to the Sun in Virgo: just as Mary of Nazareth was born when the Sun was in Cancer, so the birth of the other Mary, Mary of Bethlehem (she who stood under the Cross at the Crucifixion of Christ Jesus) was born when the Sun was in the middle of Virgo. The designation by which she is known, the Blessed Virgin Mary, is true on a cosmic level, because the Sun was in the middle of Virgo. We can think of the sign of Virgo in connection with the Blessed Virgin Mary.

Coming now to Libra: the most significant event that took place when the Sun was in Libra was the Baptism in the Jordan. This was the start of Christ's ministry. At this point in time he became the God-Man, the judge of human existence here on Earth. In this quality of the Baptism, signified by the descent of the Spirit in the form of the dove, awakening new life, we can sense the finding of a new balance between heaven and Earth. The Baptism in the Jordan was the beginning of the working of the new Law. Instead of the Law of the Old Testament, "An eye for an eye, a tooth for a tooth," we find the new Law which is that of the forgiveness of sins. As Christ said, "If you forgive those who trespass against you, so will your sins be forgiven." This is the setting-up of a new balance between heaven and Earth. The Sun in Libra at the Baptism in the Jordan signified the beginning of the new dispensation, the Christian law of justice based upon mercy and forgiveness.

Looking at the life of Christ, we find that a remarkable event took place when the Sun was in Scorpio. Many events in Christ's ministry occurred when the Sun was in Scorpio, but the most significant was the raising from the dead of the youth of Nain. This event took place around nine o'clock on Monday morning, November 13, in the year AD 30. Christ came with about thirty disciples down the hill to the little town of Nain. Just at that moment a funeral procession passed through the city gates. The coffin of the boy who was to be buried was being carried out of the city. He was about twelve years old, the son of a rich widow of Nain, who was one of the holy women. Christ Jesus halted the procession and commanded that the coffin be opened. Taking a twig of hyssop, sprinkling it with water upon the corpse, and praying to the Father in heaven, he raised the child from the dead. In the raising up to new life through this miracle that took place when the Sun was in Scorpio, we see the overcoming of the Scorpion's sting of death.

Coming now to the Archer, we find that the divine birth of Jesus of Nazareth as described in the Gospel of Luke took place when the Sun was in the middle of sidereal Sagittarius. This birth must be distinguished from the birth of Jesus as described in the Gospel of Matthew, who was visited by the three wise men from the East. Here it is a matter of the birth of Jesus of Nazareth as described in the Gospel of Luke, who was visited by the shepherds. This birth took place on the night after the Sabbath, the night of December 6/7 in the year 2 BC, toward midnight, as the Sun was in the middle of Sagittarius. This divine birth, then, took place when the Sun was in Sagittarius, whereas the other birth, connected with the visit of the Magi, took place when the Sun was in Pisces. Contemplating this birth of the Messiah in Sagittarius, we may think of the image for Sagittarius, that of the centaur. In Greek mythology this is connected with the figure of Cheiron, who was the wise teacher of the Argonauts, instructor of the great Greek heroes. He was the wise teacher and healer. This archetype was fulfilled in the being of Jesus of Nazareth, who was called the Saviour. Saviour actually means healer. Just as John the Baptist is so called because he baptized, Jesus is called the Saviour because he healed. Everywhere he went, he laid his hands on the sick. In almost every town he visited, he healed the sick and taught the people of Israel. So we find this archetype of the centaur, the wise being of Cheiron as depicted in Greek mythology, actually finding its fulfillment in the life of Jesus of Nazareth.

Looking now at the sign of Capricorn, we find that one of the most significant events in the life of Christ that took place with the Sun in Capricorn was the Wedding at Cana. This wedding in the small town

of Cana took place on Wednesday morning, December 28 in the year
AD 29, when the Sun was at around 8 degrees in Capricorn. In this
event there transpired the transformation of substance. At the
wedding, Christ had the responsibility of providing the wine. He had
not brought any wine with him. When the wine was asked for, he told
the servants to bring six vessels of water, which he then blessed; and
when the guests drank this water, they tasted wine. As they drank
there took place a miraculous communion with the being of Christ.
This was the first of his miracles, of the seven miracles described in
the Gospel of John. There were about one hundred guests at the
wedding, mainly friends and relatives of Jesus, and through this
miraculous communion they recognized him to be the Messiah. This
event of the transubstantiation—the transformation of water into
wine—was the precursor of the octave of this event at the Last
Supper, when the communion with bread and wine took place.

In the figure of Capricorn, which strives from the depths (older
depictions show the sea-goat with its tail in the water arising out of
the water toward the Spirit) we have something of an image of this
miracle of the transformation of water into wine. Through Christ
the fire of the Spirit descended into the water. As the Son of God he
was able to reinstate the primal condition of water as described at
the beginning of Genesis: "The spirit of God hovered above the face
of the waters." The fire of divine love entered into the water, and
when the disciples drank it, it tasted as wine. They were filled with
this fire of divine love. Here we see something of the deeper significance of the sign of Capricorn, which has to do with the raising up
of the material to the spiritual.

Lastly, the sign of Aquarius. The most profound miracle that took
place in the sign of Aquarius was the Feeding of the Five Thousand,
which was followed that night by the Walking on the Water. In both
events, but especially in the Walking on the Water, something of the
power of the Waterman, Aquarius, became manifest through Christ
revealing himself, already partly in his resurrection body, at that
time in his ministry. The Feeding of the Five Thousand occurred on
the afternoon of January 29 in the year AD 31, and that night, January 29/30, the Walking on the Water took place, with the Sun at
around 11 degrees of sidereal Aquarius.

By relating to events in the life of Christ in connection with the signs of the zodiac, we find a wonderful higher meaning and symbolism. Through this there is a lifting up, a raising up of the symbolism of the zodiac to a higher level, one that can be understood in terms of the Christian religion. When we allow these wonderful pictures from the life of Christ to arise in connection with their cosmic background, they enable us to gain a feeling for the signs of the zodiac on a new level. Furthermore, there is also the profound mystery of the twelve disciples summoned by Christ—he as the incarnation of the Spirit Sun on Earth with these twelve human beings, each related to one of the signs of the zodiac, through whom he was able to work in his mission of healing and teaching. The culmination of this mystery of the Logos, the Divine Word, the Spirit of the Sun, working through the twelve disciples as a mirror of the passage of the Sun through the twelve signs of the zodiac, was fulfilled in the holy mystery of the Last Supper. This event is the central mystery with regard to acquiring an understanding of the relationship of Christ to the zodiac. For those who would like to follow this up, I have written about this in *Christian Hermetic Astrology: The Star of the Magi and the Life of Christ*.[3] Here we find a seed impulse for raising up the animal circle to the human circle (*Tierkreis* to *Menschenkreis*), which signifies a raising up of the ancient astrology to a new and higher level.[4]

3. Robert Powell, *Christian Hermetic Astrology: The Star of the Magi and the Life of Christ* (Gt. Barrington, MA: SteinerBooks, 1998).

4. See Robert Powell, *Chronicle of the Living Christ* (Gt. Barrington, MA: SteinerBooks, 1996), for the specification of the dates mentioned in this chapter.

The Start of the
New Millennium

IN ORDER TO GAIN A BROADER PERSPECTIVE of the future, we can ask: What is the purpose of the whole of evolution here on the Earth? This is expressed in the last book of the Bible, in the Apocalypse, which describes the arising of a New Heaven and a New Earth—the holy city of Jerusalem. If we hold this in mind, we see that this future goal is to be arrived at only through the working of the Christ Impulse. The whole book of Revelation, the Apocalypse, is really a series of great images which speak to us of the two paths that open up to humanity: the path with Christ to the heavenly Jerusalem, to the goal of humanity, and the path down into the abyss, which is described in terms of all the great trials that are presented. Against this background, we can appreciate the value of trying to come to an understanding of the Christ Impulse; we begin to see the significance of finding out more about the life of Christ: not just the dates when events took place in the life of Christ, but—having found the dates—the cosmic configurations in the life of Christ at the time of these events. These cosmic configurations can speak to us, especially as they act as active impulses through the whole of history.

By way of illustration, let us consider the fact that we celebrate our birthday each year on the date on which we are born. Is there any deeper significance to this? We are one year older, of course, but there is certainly a deeper significance to it. The Sun takes one year to move around the zodiac, and therefore on one's birthday, the Sun returns to the same position in the zodiac that it occupied at birth. If we take the working of the stars seriously, this means that each human being chooses to incarnate upon the Earth when the Sun is at a certain position in the zodiac. For example, Rudolf Steiner chose to be born when the Sun was in the middle of sidereal Aquarius. He came into incarnation with a tremendous Aquarian impulse. We can imagine his higher being in the image of the Waterman, pouring out the waters of wisdom, preparing the way for the Aquarian Age. Each year, when the Sun returns to the same position as at birth, it means that the higher self, which is connected with the Sun, is able to radiate through more strongly than at any other time of the year. For this reason the birthday is actually a special day. Rudolf Steiner even indicated how significant it is that one celebrates a person's birthday, because his or her higher self—borne by the Guardian Angel—is especially close at that time, and truly a kind of spiritual festival takes place.

With regard to the life of Christ, we spoke earlier of the birth of the two Jesus children: the one described in the Gospel of Matthew, who was visited by the three kings, having been born on March 5, 6 BC, when the Sun was in the middle of sidereal Pisces, and the Jesus child described in the Gospel of Luke, who was visited by the shepherds, having been born on the evening of December 6 in the year 2 BC, when the Sun was in the middle of sidereal Sagittarius. This latter figure is the being who lived 33⅓ years and passed through death on the Cross. His whole life was a living out of this higher image of Sagittarius as the teacher and healer.

Each year when the Sun returns to this position in the middle of Sagittarius, we have a commemoration of the birthday of Jesus, of the divine birth of Jesus. In this event we can recall something of the accomplishment of his divine mission. Because of the precession of the equinoxes, the Sun returns to the middle of sidereal Sagittarius a little bit later each year. So it is no longer on the evening of December 6 that the Sun returns to the middle of Sagittarius. At present it is on January 1 each year. We can think every New Year's Eve, when at midnight the church bells ring to herald the New Year, of a hidden or deeper significance to this celebration. It is a celebrating of the birth of Jesus of Nazareth in a cosmic sense, when the Sun returns to the same position in the zodiac as at his birth. And on January 1 in the year 2000, the Sun returned to the position where it was at his birth for the 2,000th time. Therefore the transition to the new millennium was also the 2,000th birthday anniversary of Jesus of Nazareth. This draws to our attention something of the special significance of this event, something we would not know about if we did not know when the birth took place.

There are many astrologers, clairvoyants, and prophets of doom who have prophesied all kinds of terrible things. For example, half of California is supposed to disappear. What are we to make of such prophecies of destruction, earthquakes, catastrophes, and so on? We cannot just dismiss them out of hand, but we need to look at them in a particular context. Generally speaking, it is not possible to predict the future exactly, for otherwise there would be no freedom. There are always choices at work. Nevertheless, it is possible to say that the whole of humanity will have to pass through very significant trials. To stand up to a trial successfully means to develop new spiritual faculties; not to stand up to a trial results in a catastrophe of some kind—signifying a 'punishment'.

There are basically three kinds of trial and three kinds of punishment which we can think of in connection with the future. How is it possible to say this? If we look back to the beginning of humanity's history here on the Earth, we find the event known as the Fall, which is described in the Book of Genesis as the Temptation of Lucifer and the Expulsion from Paradise. The Fall from Paradise was the expulsion from the spiritual sphere in which humanity at that time lived, a humanity harmoniously united with the whole of nature. It was then that human incarnations upon the Earth began. What is described here are the three primal curses that were placed upon humanity as a consequence of the Fall. These are spoken of in the Book of Genesis as toil, suffering, and death. So this is a fundamental reality of life on Earth: toil of some kind—in order to live we have to work; suffering of some kind—no human being who lives on Earth passes through life without going through suffering; and there is no human being who can escape death. These are the three primal curses placed upon humanity, which are in fact a blessing. For example, through death we are reunited with the spiritual world. It would be far more unbearable if death did not exist. Moreover, through suffering we learn compassion. In experiencing pain and suffering ourselves we are able to experience compassion for other people's suffering. Lastly, through toil, through having to do things, we develop spiritually. We become spiritually active rather than just being passive. So we can say that these three primal curses of humanity are in fact blessings in disguise.

The spiritual path that was always taught through the ancient mysteries is the positive acceptance of the three primal curses, signifying their inward transformation. Thus, a positive and willing acceptance of toil—voluntary toil—is entailed in taking up a path of meditation. This means one labours for the sake of the spirit, and one does this voluntarily in such a way that one positively transforms toil. Along the path of spiritual development one encounters trials. And in a spirit of positive acceptance, one voluntarily takes upon oneself suffering. Hence it is possible to positively transform suffering as a deepening of the spiritual path. And lastly, the positive acceptance of death—passing through death consciously and voluntarily—is initiation, which is the goal of the spiritual path.

The non-acceptance of these basic realities of life leads to catastrophe. The non-acceptance of toil leads to war and strife between human beings, for in war one person or a group of people tries to acquire something, not through honest labour, but through conquering others. The non-acceptance of suffering leads to epidemics of some kind or other, which come from the periphery of our environment. One need not understand 'epidemic' simply in the sense of illness. There are all kinds of epidemics. There can be an epidemic of a crazy idea, of a cult, or of some kind of perverse feeling, all of which can lead to some peculiar form of mass movement. Naturally, it can also manifest as illness. Thirdly, the non-acceptance of death leads, in nature, to the phenomenon of earthquakes. The connection between the human being and nature is very deep, and if we try to feel what the aim of so many people is—to avoid death, because they fear it—we find that the fear works back into nature and can subsequently arise as an earthquake. The quaking of the Earth is an expression of human beings' fear.

Three kinds of catastrophe, three kinds of punishment, which come again and again in the course of history: war, epidemic, and earthquake. Something of this is also indicated in Christ's words to the disciples in the Gospel of Matthew, when he speaks of the coming of wars and earthquakes. Let us now try to understand the significance of this. In the first place, war can be on different levels. It need not just be war on the physical level; it can be war on the etheric level or on the astral level; it can be war between nations or between groups; it can be war between the sexes. Similarly, epidemics can take place on different levels: on the level of thought, on the level of feeling, or on the level where one actually has physical illness. Thirdly, earthquakes can also take place on different levels. A physical earthquake is an eruption from below, but a revolution in society is also an earthquake coming from below, disrupting and throwing everything into chaos. Spiritually speaking, there are three kinds of gesture or movement here. War is always an impulse working from a central point outward, like a battering ram, bringing destruction in its wake. Epidemic is an impulse working from the periphery inward, bringing destruction from without. And earthquake, the third kind of catastrophe, is a movement from below disrupting everything.

In the course of the twentieth century there have already been two world wars, and World War II especially can be regarded as a sign of the opening of one of the seals spoken of in the Apocalypse. In the AIDS epidemic we can again see an apocalyptic sign. Moreover, many clairvoyants have predicted the coming of a cataclysmic earthquake, which will be a third sign. All of these potential future catastrophes, however, can be transformed through human effort. Thus it is impossible to say with absolute certainty "an earthquake will occur on such and such a date in the future," for it is conceivable that human beings can transform this.

Looking now from another point of view at these three kinds of catastrophe resulting from failure with respect to three kinds of trial, there is another perspective that I would like to briefly indicate. As a consequence of the Fall, the human being's lower astral nature was intensely activated. Through the working of powerful passions in the wake of the Fall (this was in the period of Earth evolution prior to Atlantis, the evolution that took place on the ancient continent of Lemuria)—the destruction of Lemuria was brought about through a great catastrophe, a fire catastrophe. This fire catastrophe was an expression of the fiery passions at work in human beings' astral nature as a consequence of the Fall.

Then came the Atlantean civilization, which unfolded through seven ages or civilizations on the great continent that was situated between America and Europe. At the end of these seven civilizations a great catastrophe submerged Atlantis. The destruction of Atlantis took place through a water catastrophe, the flood. Here again, it was on account of forces that were being awakened in human beings but were misused, forces to do with the human being's relationship with nature. The misuse of nature forces brought on the great flood, which is also spoken of in the Bible. There it is described how Noah rescued a small group of people and led them over from Atlantis to start a new culture. This post-Atlantean civilization began in the Age of Cancer with the civilization of ancient India. Noah was the one human being who preserved spiritual memory going back to the past of the Earth. A consequence of these catastrophes for those human beings upon the Earth undergoing them was that to a certain extent they became somewhat 'deranged' and lost the memory of belonging to a spiritual world. Memory became something other than it had been prior to the Fall. Noah was the one human being who retained fully conscious memory of the past, and Noah's Ark is the symbol of this continuity of consciousness that Noah possessed. Therefore he was able to transmit the spiritual mysteries of the past and bring them forward again as a seed for a new civilization that started on the continent of India in the Age of Cancer.

Following the ancient Indian civilization there arose the civilization of ancient Persia, which was the main civilization in the Age of Gemini. Then came the civilization of Egypt and Babylon in the Age of Taurus, followed by Greek and Roman culture in the Age of Aries. Now, in the present Age of Pisces, European civilization is the central civilization, this being the fifth great civilization since the destruction of Atlantis. In the sixth age, the Age of Aquarius, the region of Russia will be the focus of the central spiritual impulse, and then in the Age of Capricorn, the North American continent will be the guiding center of world civilization. It is possible to speak of a great catastrophe that will occur at the end of these seven civilizations. Just as a fire catastrophe destroyed Lemuria, and the Flood, the water catastrophe, destroyed Atlantis, so there will be an air catastrophe, which will signify the destruction of our civilization as we know it. The air catastrophe will come around the end of the seventh civilization, the American civilization, which corresponds to the Age of Capricorn.

What can we understand concerning this future air catastrophe? What does it signify? The catastrophes of fire in Lemuria, water in Atlantis, and of air at the end of our present civilization, mirror the trials we undergo on the spiritual path: the trial by fire, the trial of purification for which we must develop courage in order to pass; the trial by water, which requires the force of self-mastery in order to pass; and the trial by air, which calls for the development of spiritual presence of mind in order to pass.

What does this mean, the air catastrophe? Air is something we all have in common. It actually unites us, but more and more we can see that air is becoming a problem for our civilization. We need only think of the ozone holes at the North and South Poles, and of increasing air pollution. But these are only physical manifestations. In the future there will develop something we can call the magical use of air. Then the air will become more and more the domain of battle and struggle between human beings. This will lead to the war of all against all. Air is the element in which our astral nature lives. Our astral nature is basically full of egotism. This will become stronger and stronger. We can see all the signs of this in our present-day civilization: how self-will is becoming more and more powerful. Future battles will take place between individuals using magical forces, making use of winds, gases, poisonous vapors, and all kinds of destructive elements in the air, which will eventually lead to the great catastrophe when the winds will be completely out of control. Anybody who has experienced a hurricane or typhoon knows what a terrifying event this is. The future air catastrophe will lead to the destruction of our civilization. We can see that what is called for in taking up the spiritual path is the willing acceptance of the trials— fire, water, and air—and the development of the qualities that are called for to withstand these trials: purity and courage to pass through the fire trial, self-control, self-mastery for the water trial, and spiritual presence of mind for the air trial.

On at least one occasion, Rudolf Steiner referred to the possibility that this war of all against all could come now in our time. In other words, it could occur not long after the end of the twentieth century, two ages before it should take place. This is based on an understanding of something very special that is coming to pass in our time. The population of humanity is now around six billion. According to the ancient Persian tradition (as expressed in its account of creation, the *Bundahisn*), God created a total of six billion human souls. If this is so,[1] then at the present time, for the first time in the history of humanity, all human souls are incarnated upon the Earth. One could ask: Why is this? What is the significance of this? This is in order to meet and pass through a particular trial that is coming. The question is: What is this trial that is coming to meet humanity?

We find in the life of Christ a key to understanding the present moment in history, for the life of Christ, especially the days from the Baptism in the Jordan to the Mystery of Golgotha, was like an embryonic period, a seed implanted, from which the future course of world history is fructified, leading in a positive sense to the arising of the future Jerusalem. Everything Christ did has a higher significance. As he himself said, "Heaven and Earth will pass away, but my words will not pass away." Every deed he fulfilled is of eternal significance. He is present with us throughout all of Earth evolution as a seed force that will grow and grow. The period between the Baptism and the Mystery of Golgotha can be likened to the period between conception and birth. We could say that the Risen One was born on Easter Sunday through the Resurrection. This event actually shows us the goal of evolution. The conception of this being Christ Jesus took place at the Baptism in the Jordan. From the Baptism in the Jordan on September 23, AD 29 through to Easter Sunday on April 5, AD 33 is a period of 3½ years or 1,290 days. It is also the period mentioned by Daniel in the last chapter of the Book of Daniel.

Each one of these days was a preparation for the unfolding of the future history of humanity. The key to this unfolding of the Christ impulse is that one day in the life of Christ corresponds to 29½

---

1. The *Bundahisn* is, as far as I know, the only Sacred Book that specifies the number of souls created by God. Of course, the figure of six billion souls referred to in this text might be figurative rather than literal.

years of history. Those familiar with astronomy will know that this is the period required by Saturn to make one orbit of the sidereal zodiac. Saturn requires almost exactly 29½ years for this orbit of the sidereal zodiac. The first day following on from the Baptism corresponds to the first 29½ years of history, the second day to the second 29½ years, and so on. We can actually determine when the end of the Earth will take place in this way: that is, 1,290 times this Saturn rhythm of 29½ years, which takes us to the year AD 38000. So we still have some way to go!

To show that this is not just a figure pulled from a hat, we can support it from a totally different perspective. In the Book of Revelation we find a description of the future in terms of the opening of the Seven Letters of the Seven Communities. This relates to our present seven civilizations, ours being the fifth. Then follow the Seven Seals, relating to the seven civilizations that will follow after the air catastrophe at the end of our seven civilizations. Then come the Seven Trumpets, signifying a sequence of seven still more far-distant future civilizations, leading to the end of Earth evolution. Then come the Seven Vials of Wrath, which indicates the time after the end of Earth evolution. The period of the Seven Vials of Wrath signifies the *kamaloka* of the Earth at the end of Earth evolution. Just as every human being passes through kamaloka or purgatory at the end of his or her life on Earth, so the whole Earth will pass through this period of purgatory, and will re-emerge subsequently as the Heavenly Jerusalem.

In connection with the precession of the equinoxes, each age lasts 2,160 years. Our present cultural age of Pisces began in the year AD 1414. This is the fifth age. The fifth, sixth, and seventh—another three ages—will lead us to the end of this period of cultural evolution. So we have here 3 x 2,160 = 6,480 years. Adding this to 1414, we come to 7894 as the time of the end of our seven civilizations, the time of the great air catastrophe, the War of All against All. This indicates the end—at approximately 8000—of the period of the seven letters described in the Apocalypse. Then come the seven seals, which takes us through a further 7 x 2,160 = 15,120 years, bringing us up to 7,894 + 15,120 = 23014. Lastly, there follow a further 7 x 2,160 = 15,120 years, which added to 23014 brings us to 38134.

Rounding this off, we arrive here from a totally different point of view at the same date for the end of Earth evolution, insofar as it is possible to measure it in terms of years in relation to the precession of the equinoxes. So we see in these 1,290 days belonging to the life of Christ the seed or embryo of everything that is to unfold into the future. We could ask: Where do we stand now, at the present point in time, in relation to the embryo, the life of Christ?

At present we are in the period described in the Gospels as the Forty Days of Temptation in the Wilderness. Historically, the period of temptation started on the evening of the Sabbath, Friday, October 21, AD 29. The interval between the Baptism and the start of the period of temptation was 28 days. Taking this correspondence (one day = 29½ years; 28 x 29½ = 836 years), we must then add this to the year AD 33, which is the starting point—AD 33 being the year of the Mystery of Golgotha. In terms of our calendar, the beginning of the temptation of humanity started in the year AD 869 (= 33 + 836).

Interestingly, this was the year of the eighth Ecumenical Council, which took place in Constantinople. It was actually the fourth council to take place in Constantinople. Here occurred the beginning of the split or separation between the Eastern and the Western Churches. The Eastern Church holds the point of view that from this time onward the force of materialism, combined with a lack of understanding of the human being's spiritual nature, came into the Western Church. A darkening, a period of temptation, began in the year AD 869.

At that time Saturn was in sidereal Sagittarius. Every time Saturn returns to sidereal Sagittarius we have a further 'day' in these 40 days of temptation. If we take the forty days and reckon 40 x 29½ = 1,178 years, and then add this to AD 869, we find that the end of the period of temptation is in the year 2047, in the middle of the present century. We are still right in the thick of it. We can be still more precise. By the last day in the wilderness, the fortieth day, Christ had overcome the temptations. In the Gospel of Matthew and the Gospel of Luke only three temptations are described. These three temptations are also related to what I described earlier as the three basic trials or the three basic punishments. The overcoming of these three temptations is at the same time the overcoming of the forces of destruction. Fundamentally, the whole of history is the story of humanity's wrestling with the three temptations. The period of temptation culminated on the thirty-ninth day. The temptations lasted throughout almost the whole of the forty days, but the three temptations described in the Gospel of Matthew and the Gospel of Luke took place on the thirty-seventh, thirty-eighth, and thirty-ninth days. The 40th day was the day on which, as described in the Gospels, "angels came and ministered unto him." Going back one Saturn revolution from 2047, we arrive at the start of the last day, the fortieth day, in the year 2018, when Saturn will next be in Sagittarius. We are now in the period of the thirty-ninth day. The thirty-ninth day commenced with Saturn in Sagittarius in 1988. At the present time Saturn is progressing through the signs and will pass around the zodiac to be again in sidereal Sagittarius in the year 2018.

What took place on the thirty-ninth day in the wilderness? It was the day of the third temptation, the temptation of turning stones into bread. This is essentially the temptation of materialism; that is, trying to take hold of the material and make it one's spiritual possession, which amounts to turning stones into bread. Christ's reply was, "Man does not live by bread alone, but by every word from the mouth of God." In other words, he directs our attention to the spiritual, to the divine Word that proceeds from the spiritual realm. This is the challenge, to place the spiritual above the material. It is interesting that Christ says "Man does not live by bread alone," for it is clear that we do need bread. We need the material, and we have to respect the material world, but it should not be the sole source of our attention.

This third temptation is now building up to a climax. It is this trial which we—the whole of humanity—will pass through, that is presented by the tempter described in the Gospel of Matthew as Satan, the being named Ahriman in the Persian tradition. It is he who presents this temptation of turning stones into bread. The challenge humanity faces is that we are now living in the period leading up to the year 2018, that of the incarnation of Ahriman, or, in traditional Christian terms, the incarnation of Antichrist.

A source of understanding of this trial or temptation is found in the thirteenth chapter of the Apocalypse, where Satan, known in the

Christian tradition as Antichrist, is called the Beast. The Beast is described as coming to rule upon the Earth for a period of 3½ years. Interestingly, this is exactly the period of Christ's ministry. It is also said that the Beast is assisted by another being, who is described as a two-horned beast, a false prophet able to wield magical powers and call down fire from heaven. This second being is a source or vehicle for the inspiration of black magic, the inspiration of the Sun Demon, who is called in the Jewish mystery tradition *Sorath*. This word has the letters Samech, Vau, Resh and Tau. Moreover, each letter in the Hebrew alphabet has a numerical value: Samech = 60, Vau = 6, Resh = 200, Tau = 400. If we add these values together we have the number 666, which is referred to in the Book of Revelation as the number of the Beast. The two-horned beast, Sorath, works in history in the rhythm of 666 years. Around the time of the year, AD 666, Sorath worked very powerfully in an attempt to bring— already at that time—something resembling what we now have as modern science. Sorath worked by way of inspiration especially in the Academy of Gondishapur in Persia. But the working of this influence at that time was weakened through Mohammed, through Islam, which effectively curtailed the influence of the Academy of Gondishapur.

The influence of Sorath culminated a second time in the period around (2 x 666 =) AD 1332. At this time, in the fourteenth century, a negative inspiration again worked especially powerfully, leading to the destruction of the Order of the Knights Templar. The third time is now, around (3 x 666 =) 1998. Here there is a new influence of Sorath at work. Thus Ahriman, or Satan, who is presenting the third temptation, is assisted now by Sorath, whose negative inspiration is directed toward a human being referred to in the Apocalypse as the prophet, the two-horned beast, and here we are confronted with the force of black magic. We are living in very challenging times! We are called upon to understand the working of these trials and temptations, and to seek ways to overcome them.

What I have depicted regarding the times in which we are living would be rather a bleak picture if I did not portray something else that we need to take into consideration. This is connected with the Second Coming of Christ, which is an event that brings the possibility of overcoming these negative forces and influences. This event will also work powerfully into the whole realm of nature. Although from one point of view there is the possibility that natural catastrophes can occur as a result of human beings' misdeeds and wrong attitudes with respect to nature, these can be balanced out by the working of the Second Coming of Christ, which takes place not on the physical plane but in the etheric aura of the Earth, and so takes effect in the whole world of nature. On the one hand, exacerbated by the misdeeds and wrong attitudes of humanity, an extremely chaotic element is entering into weather conditions, and on the other there is a very powerful harmonizing and healing influence taking place in nature, bringing exactly the opposite. Humanity stands in the midst of a tremendous struggle.

Now at the start of the new millennium, a very special positive event approaches. It is possible for everyone to make a connection with this event, which is bound up with the Second Coming of Christ. How is this possible? When the human being dies, the physical body is laid aside as the corpse, and the etheric body, the body of life that permeates the physical body, separates from the physical body together with the soul and the spirit of the human being. As we have spoken of already, at this moment the human being is no longer living in his or her physical body but in the etheric body. He or she experiences a panorama of all the events that took place in the life just ended. In other words, the etheric body is the bearer of all the experiences we undergo between birth and death. This experience lasts for about three days, until the etheric body dissolves into the etheric cosmos. In the case of Christ Jesus, however, his etheric body did not dissolve at his death, but was preserved. It contains all the events Christ Jesus lived through between birth and death. And as we said earlier, this was a period of exactly 33⅓ years. Since the Mystery of Golgotha in the year AD 33, this etheric organism of Christ has been working in a rhythm of 33⅓ years, working primarily from cosmic realms. The significance of the Second Coming of Christ is the return of his etheric organism to work into the Earth's etheric aura. This etheric organism of Christ contains the images of all the events in his life. Already from the year 1899, this new working began to take place. Rudolf Steiner was able to read from this etheric aura—this etheric organism of Christ—and so to describe many events in the lectures that he entitled the *Fifth Gospel*. The four Gospels, which describe events in the life of Christ, were also drawn from this Fifth Gospel. The Fifth Gospel, the etheric organism of Christ, is the source also of the other Gospels. It is with this Gospel that we are now able to connect. Earlier in history some individuals who underwent a special period of purification were able to come into connection with the etheric organism of Christ. For example, St Francis of Assisi, who bore the stigmata, lived in visions stemming from the life of Christ, and Anne Catherine Emmerich, who also bore the stigmata, also lived in continuous connection with the etheric organism of Christ.

Now, increasingly in our time, it is possible to enter into a relationship with the etheric body of Christ. Obviously it is a help if one begins to think about the life of Christ, to actively imagine and to live with the scenes depicted in this life. In looking at this rhythm, we find something very interesting. From the Birth up to the Resurrection was a period of 33⅓ years. And the period from the Baptism in the Jordan up to the Mystery of Golgotha was 3½ years. At the time of the Baptism in the Jordan, as described in the Gospel of Matthew, Jesus was almost 30 years of age. In fact, he was 29 years and 9½ months of age. From this age onward, during this period of 3½ years, the real unfolding of the mission of Christ Jesus took place. Thus this period, the last 3½ years of each 33⅓-year period, has a special significance. If we follow this rhythm through history, from the Mystery of Golgotha in the year AD 33, we arrive after 56 33⅓ year rhythms at the year 1899, which marks the beginning of the New Age. The term New Age actually signifies the renewed working-in of the etheric body of Christ. And it was precisely at this time that Rudolf Steiner underwent his initiation—analogous to Saul's at the gates of Damascus, whereby he became Paul. Up to that point, Rudolf Steiner had not especially occupied himself with Christianity. Then, in 1899, as he describes in his *Autobiography*, he underwent a profound inner experience of the Mystery of Golgotha. This was possible at that moment because it marked the completion of a 33⅓-year cycle. One can date this even more exactly to September in the year 1899. Then followed the first rhythm of

33⅓ years after the New Age commenced, leading up to January 8, 1933. The next rhythm of 33⅓ years leads up to May 9, 1966. And then followed the third period of 33⅓ years since the start of the New Age, leading up to September 6 in the year 1999.[2] We have seen that the most important period in the 33⅓-year cycle is the last 3½ years, which means for us the 3½ years from February 24, 1996 through to September 6, 1999.[3] During this time an opportunity was presented for entering into an experience in the etheric realm of all the events that took place day by day in the life of Christ between the Baptism and the Mystery of Golgotha. Such an experience is a most powerful source of help in the coming time of trial and temptation.

As I said earlier, the whole West Coast is of very special significance with regard to this event. We may recall that around the end of the 33⅓-year period in 1966, the hippie movement was drawing inspiration from the West Coast. Behind this stood something of a renewed Christian impulse, which was unfortunately derailed by all kinds of other things, the drug epidemic for example, and so lost its real impetus as a potential for changing our culture. Something else of special inspiration stemming from the West Coast is possible now, because the Pacific is the area whence the Moon departed from the Earth. The Earth's etheric aura extends up to the Moon, and so the Pacific area is one where the Christ impulse working in the etheric aura of the Earth takes its point of departure. It then moves in a wave-like movement eastward, raying out from the West Coast. On the West Coast there is a streaming-in of new spiritual impulses, which then weave eastward across North America and further thence Europe and on to the rest of the world. Here on the West Coast it is a very special time at the start of the new millennium, when there is a possibility for new spiritual impulses to come streaming in, impulses that can help in the struggle now taking place in humanity and in the realm of nature. Knowing such mysteries connected with the unfolding of the Christ Impulse,

2. See Robert Powell, *The Christ Mystery* (Fair Oaks, CA: Rudolf Steiner College Press, 1999), for a discussion of the 33⅓-year rhythm.
    3. Ibid.

it becomes possible to enter into these events on a much deeper level.

We will look next at the coming millennium and consider the possibilities for what will take place in connection with the coming new revelation of Sophia.[4]

4. The dates given above are presented in a more comprehensive way in *Chronicle of the Living Christ*, referred to on page 41.

The
Sophianic
Millennium

WE ARE AT THE START of a new millennium. This is a tremendous turning-point in evolution, some 2,000 years having elapsed since the divine birth in Bethlehem. On the first evening I spoke about the perspective of the divine wisdom that was cultivated by the Egyptians and Babylonians as the wisdom of the stars, which we could call Astro-Sophia or *astrosophy*. This was during the Age of Taurus. Then came the Age of Aries and the birth of the Greek and Roman civilizations. This was the time of the emerging of Philo-Sophia or *philosophy*, signifying another relationship to Sophia than that of the Egyptians and Babylonians. In our time, in the Age of Pisces, through Anthropo-Sophia or *anthroposophy*, there is again a new and different relationship of humanity to Sophia. All of this is leading toward the direct meeting with the being of Sophia in the next age, the Aquarian Age—the meeting with the being who is the heart of all true culture. The Sophianic millennium, as the coming thousand years has been called, is a time of turning toward this new revelation of Sophia. From different points of view it is possible to think of this coming millennium as a time of the unfolding impulse of Sophia.

Up until recently, Sophia has remained more or less concealed in the West. For historical reasons Christianity inherited the Jewish patriarchal tradition. This has meant a more masculine-oriented perspective of evolution, and consequently the ancient pre-Christian devotion to the Divine Feminine receded into the background. We need only think of the fact that the mysteries of Eleusis in Greece, the cult center dedicated to Demeter, the Mother, became closed, and that the cult of Isis celebrated in the Egyptian mysteries became forgotten. Only now, in the New Age that has started in the twentieth century, is there a re-awakening in the West to the being of Sophia.

A relationship to the being of Sophia was cultivated on a devotional level throughout the centuries in the Eastern Church, particularly in the Russian Orthodox Church. At the beginning of the twentieth century, especially through the work of the Russian philosopher Vladimir Solovyov, there came to birth what is called Sophiology, the philosophical and theological study of Sophia. This was taken up, amongst other, by two Russian Orthodox priests, Pavel Florensky and Sergei Bulgakov, who were stimulated in their Sophiological work by the inspiration they received from Solovyov.[1] Solovyov himself had three mystical experiences of Sophia during his life. From these experiences was born within him the seed impulse for Sophiology. We can understand something of these connections and why this relationship to the being of Sophia lived and developed in Russia when we recall that the Russian civilization will come to the fore in the Aquarian Age, when the Sophia revelation will come into its own. Thus, in the East there is preparation for the coming age of Aquarius, just as there is in the West through the work of spiritual teachers like Rudolf Steiner, and it is very helpful to build bridges between the East and the West with regard to this awakening to Sophia.

In the West, although a conscious relationship to Sophia has receded into the background, there has remained—at least within the Roman Catholic Church—a devotion to the being of Mary, who has a very close relationship to the Divine Wisdom, Sophia. In fact one of the fundamental ideas of Sophiology is that the Divine Wisdom, Holy Sophia, incarnated into the being of Mary.[2] This is set forth in the work of Florensky. The outstanding figure in the whole history of Russian Sophiology, who can be regarded as a culmination

---

1. Thomas Schipflinger, *Sophia-Maria* (York Beach, ME: Samuel Weiser, 1997), gives an excellent summary of Russian Sophiology and the works of Solovyov, Florensky, and Bulgakov
2. Ibid.

of this stream, is the Russian Sophiologist Valentin Tomberg, who left Russia about the time of the Revolution, coming to the West after a stay in Estonia, living first in Holland, then for a short time in Germany, settling finally in England. He brought the central—what can be regarded as the crowning—teaching of Sophiology.[3]

In Christian theology the great teaching developed by the Church Fathers was the doctrine of the Holy Trinity. There is no clear theology concerning the Holy Trinity in the New Testament. It was developed by the Church Fathers. The central teaching of the Russian Sophiologist Valentin Tomberg is that just as there is a Holy Trinity of Father, Son, and Holy Spirit, so there is a Divine Feminine Trinity, of Mother (corresponding to the Father), Daughter (corresponding to the Son), and Holy Soul (corresponding to the Holy Spirit). This teaching is the key to Sophiology. It helps us understand the nature of the Divine Feminine. Valentin Tomberg's teaching on this subject is elaborated in his book *Lazarus, Come Forth.*[4] This teaching is a profound source of inspiration regarding the Divine Feminine Trinity, for it allows us to distinguish between three aspects of the Divine Feminine; and this is precisely what we need to prepare us to understand the Sophianic millennium and the new revelation of Sophia.

The Divine Feminine Trinity bears upon the whole of creation. If we look back to the time before there was any creative existence whatsoever, we can only speak of the Divine Being as a oneness. With the beginning of the creation, however, a separation occurred, a division into what one could call a male and a female pole of existence. The female pole of existence embraces all that belongs to the creation itself, whereas the part of the Divine Being that remained transcendent to creation we designate as the Father—the whole of creation itself being the Mother. The very ground of our existence is the Mother being. This was known in the mysteries of Eleusis, and

3. Valentin Tomberg, *Christ and Sophia* (Gt. Barrington, MA: SteinerBooks, 2006).

4. Valentin Tomberg, *Lazarus Come Forth* (Gt. Barrington, MA: Lindisfarne Press, 2006). See also *Meditations on the Tarot* (NY: Penguin/Tarcher, 2002), chapter 19.

the central role of the initiation there was to enter into a relationship with the Divine Mother.

We know through the Christian religion that the being of the Father bore out of himself the Son—the Son, the Logos, who is one with the Father. This is expressed in the Christian creed in the affirmation that the Son is "the only-begotten Son of the Father, one being with the Father." In terms of Sophiology, this can be expanded to include the Daughter; that is, we can speak of the being of the Son and the Daughter born of the Father and the Mother being. Here, just as we can identify the Son with Christ, so we can identify the Daughter with Sophia, with the being who was revered in the Egyptian mysteries as Isis, the Divine Wisdom. This being, who is connected with the whole starry world, is united with the stars extending throughout the far distant realms of the cosmos. And just as the Son, Christ, incarnated on Earth into the human being Jesus at the Baptism, so did the Divine Wisdom, the Daughter, Sophia, incorporate into the Virgin Mary. This mystery has remained veiled in the history of Christianity up to the present time. If we ask why this is so, it is evident that it was because it would have been too much for human beings at an earlier time in history to have focussed their attention upon the fact of the coming of two Divine beings. There is, moreover, a far-reaching difference between these two incarnations. Whereas the incarnation of Christ in Jesus was a full incarnation in the sense that Christ took hold of the complete vessel (Jesus) and transformed this vessel into pure spirit (the Resurrection), the incorporation of Sophia into Mary was only partial. In this sense it is more accurate to speak of an emanation of part of Sophia into Mary rather than an incarnation of Sophia in Mary. This emanation was of such strength that it led to the Assumption of Mary into heaven at her death—an event in the life of Mary Sophia analogous to the Ascension in the life of Jesus Christ. Our attention up to the present has been focussed primarily on the Divine incarnation of the Son, Christ, into Jesus.

The whole teaching of Jesus Christ was to open the way to the Father, to lead human beings to a connection with the Father. This was Christ's central teaching, summarized in the Lord's Prayer, the prayer given by Christ on the Mount of Beatitudes, in which we are directed to the Father with the words, "Our Father in heaven." Not only did Christ Jesus teach this, but he himself actually took this path to the Father. After the Resurrection, forty days later, he went with the disciples to the Mount of Olives. On that Thursday, Ascension Day, he climbed the Mount of Olives together with the disciples, and then ascended into heaven, becoming ever more bright and radiant until he disappeared from the disciples' sight and began his ascent to the Father. As he said to Mary Magdalene on Easter Sunday morning when he appeared to her in the Garden of the Holy Sepulchre, "Do not touch me, for I am not yet ascended to the Father." The ascent began forty days later. The central impulse of Christ at his coming 2,000 years ago was the teaching of the Father, the unveiling of the Father, leading humanity to regain consciousness of the Father.

But we may ask: What began with the renewed working-in of the etheric body of Christ in 1899, signifying, as we have said, the start of a New Age unfolding now through the renewed working of Christ in the etheric aura of the Earth? He is working now not specifically to draw our attention to the Father; rather, in this New Age of Christianity, the new Christ revelation is concerned with the being of the Mother. Already at the time of the Mystery of Golgotha, through the descent into hell after his death on the cross, Christ descended to the realm of the Mother. Christ came from the Father and descended to the Mother to re-establish a connection between the Father and Mother—a connection that had been broken through the Fall. At the time of the Fall the Mother withdrew into the realm of the underworld, and the subearthly spheres of evil came to be inserted between the heart of the Mother and humanity. It was through these spheres that Christ descended to the Mother at the time of his descent into hell.

In the present, with the second coming of Christ, a renewed descent to the Mother is taking place. This entails a conflict with evil, with all that is connected with the subearthly spheres. One aspect of this conflict is the struggle with Satan, known in the ancient Persian religion as Ahriman. A prophecy of this struggle was already announced by Zarathustra in Ancient Persia. According to Zarathustra, Ahriman, the evil twin, had long ago said to Christ: "I will win over all your followers, all human beings I shall win to worship me." And Christ, called by Zarathustra *Ahura Mazdao*, accepted the challenge, but specified a time for this encounter to take place. Now, at the present time, the conflict between Christ and Satan is reaching its culmination with the incarnation of Satan, signifying also the climax of the unfolding of the period of temptation into which humanity entered in the year AD 869 and which will be concluded by the middle of the twenty-first century.

This is not only a struggle for the souls of humanity, entailing a time of decision for each and every human being concerning his or her own innermost being. It is also a struggle for the future of the Earth and the multitude of living beings—the spirits of nature—who belong to the Mother. We need only think of every plant, every tree, sending its roots down toward the Mother: on the one hand, they strive up toward the light of the heavenly Father, and on the other down toward the kingdom of the Mother. This is an appropriate image for the kingdom of nature. In the present conflict there is a struggle also for the beings of nature. Humanity is now having to awaken to the fact that the Earth and the whole of nature depends upon us for her survival, for her salvation. In the words of Solovyov, and also of Novalis: *the human being is the messiah of nature.* As Valentin Tomberg expressed it: we have a role to fulfill toward nature analogous to that which Christ fulfills toward humanity. The whole future of the Earth depends upon our awakening to our divine responsibility toward nature. This entails an awakening to the Earth Mother, to the Being of Nature. And it is precisely the new Christ revelation that is leading to an awakening to the Mother. We see this happening now in the realm of ecology, and in other movements arising in our time. Moreover, the Divine Sophia, the Daughter, is also now beginning to become active in the context of this struggle for the Earth. The etheric aura of the Earth is like a great ocean filled with multitudes of living beings who are responsible for the plants, for the air we breathe, for everything that is living around us.

Satan's aim is to render this etheric ocean around the Earth his blood, which would make it a deadened realm. At the same time, Satan or Ahriman seeks to take hold of human blood. The counterforce to this is to be found in the working of Christ in the etheric of the human being through what is called the etherization of the blood. Every human being who makes a conscious connection to Christ Jesus participates in this etherization of the blood—we could also say this Christianizing of the blood. Blood is the bearer of the self, the 'I' of the human being. However, if one does not participate in this, if one does not find a conscious relationship to Christ, the blood may become a vehicle for the working-in of the impulse of Satan. This extends also to the kingdoms of nature. The struggle is for the very essence of the human being, for his blood, which is a theme addressed by Goethe in his drama *Faust*. The diabolical figure of Mephistopheles convinces Faust to sign a pact with him, signing with his blood—the reason for this being that blood is the bearer of the human self ('I').

Just as the Son, Christ, opened our eyes 2,000 years ago to the Father, who had hitherto been veiled, so in the coming revelation of Sophia our eyes will be opened more and more to the Mother—for there is a deep inner relationship between the Earth Mother and the Daughter, the Divine Sophia. The third member of the Divine Feminine Trinity is the Holy Soul, who weaves between the Mother in the depths and the Divine Sophia in the heights, just as the Holy Spirit weaves between the Father and the Son. The Holy Soul is the being who makes everything holy. Just as the Holy Spirit is the spiritualizer of our existence, so the Holy Soul lives in all that is holy and beautiful in our life here on Earth. We find the Holy Soul at work especially in shaping community, in building the holy foundation of human life together in family life and also in larger communities.

Trying to form a conception of the Trinity of Father, Son, and Holy Spirit raises the question: How does the Trinity relate to humanity? This relationship was formed through the incarnation of Christ in Jesus at the Baptism in the Jordan, for here a fourth being came into creation—Christ Jesus, the Messiah, a union of the divine and the human, a being other than the Father or the Son or the Holy Spirit. If we now ask how the Divine Feminine Trinity relates to humanity, we come to a second profound mystery of Sophiology: the second person of the Divine Feminine Trinity—the Daughter, Sophia—incarnated in the Virgin Mary at the Whitsun Event at the time of Pentecost. This was indicated by Valentin Tomberg in his

Studies of the New Testament. Whereas other Sophiologists have spoken of the incarnation of Sophia in Mary, Tomberg is the first Sophiologist to have indicated when and how this incarnation took place. In relation to the Divine Feminine, here is a fourth being, Mary Sophia, who builds the connection between humanity and the Divine Feminine Trinity. Mary Sophia will play an increasingly important role in the future. Partly on account of the tragedy of the separation of the Western and Eastern Church (which began at the onset of the temptation of humanity in the year AD 869), attention in the West was focussed upon the being of Mary and in the East on the being of Sophia—yet they really belong together.

There are many wonderful icons of Divine Sophia in the Russian Church. They nearly all have the same form: Sophia, Divine Wisdom, is shown as an angelic being on a throne; to her right is the Virgin Mary, to her left John the Baptist, above her Christ, and above him the Holy Book representing the Father. In this iconographic tradition of the Eastern Church John the Baptist and the Virgin Mary are depicted as the two human beings closest to Divine Sophia.

This leads us to consider another aspect of the Baptism in the Jordan in connection with the Virgin Mary, for at that time her whole being was rejuvenated through an extraordinary event. As described by Rudolf Steiner, a holy soul descended from above to unite with her, and something of the quality of the Holy Soul filled her being from this time onward. This event prepared her to become the heart of the circle of the apostles and disciples. Let us try to gain an idea of this.

We can find certain indications of Mary's relationship with the Sophianic mysteries, for example what took place on the night of the Divine birth. In her account of this event, Anne Catherine Emmerich describes how all around the Earth, as the birth of Jesus took place, the whole of nature rose up and rejoiced: a spring of water gushed forth in the cave adjacent to the birth grotto, and all around remarkable events occurred in the whole of nature. This was the response of the Mother, the Earth Mother, to the divine birth. From the depths of nature, from the womb of the Mother, the divine fire that burns in the center of the Earth—the life force sustaining all life—rose up and permeated the Virgin Mary. Just as the dove of light descended from the realm of the Father at the Baptism in the Jordan, so at the nativity the life force, the divine warmth, of the Mother ascended from the depths. Enveloped by this life-sustaining divine warmth, the Virgin Mary was able to give birth in a condition of ecstasy. She experienced no pain but only a burst of sublime joy. This union with the creative power of the Mother was a great moment in the life of the Virgin Mary, and from this time on she had an inner connection with the Mother, and through this an awareness of the whole of nature.

The Virgin Mary was a profoundly silent being. This was an outer manifestation of her transcendental consciousness. Not only was she conscious of the whole of nature, but from the Baptism on she was, through the Holy Soul, conscious of everything going on in the hearts of all those human beings around her. Every new disciple who came into the circle of the growing community was introduced to the Virgin Mary by Christ Jesus. She then took the being of this disciple into her consciousness, thus fulfilling her role as the heart of this growing community. This was a working of the Holy Soul through the Virgin Mary, who was a being of sublime purity.

A third momentous event in the Virgin Mary's life was the union with Sophia at the Whitsun Event. The apostles and disciples were gathered together in the Coenaculum on Mt. Zion on the evening before Pentecost Sunday. On that Saturday evening they came together and prayed throughout the night. During the early hours, as the sun was just beginning to rise, they heard the sound of a rushing wind. The Virgin Mary was with them. She was in a condition of transcendental ecstasy, of absolute peace and calm. At this moment the Divine Sophia incarnated into the being of Mary. This incarnation of Sophia coincided with the descent of the Holy Spirit as tongues of fire upon each of the apostles. This event signified the overcoming of the consequences of the building of the Tower of Babel, which had divided humankind through different languages and tongues. The apostles were raised to the sphere of activity of Sophia, who is able to work on the level of the different folk spirits. In a sense, she can be regarded as the heart of the folk spirits and as a true bearer of peace between different peoples and nations. At

Pentecost the souls of the apostles were elevated to the archangelic sphere, the sphere of language, and they were able to understand and speak different tongues. The Whitsun event was a revelation of Sophia, and it is this event that must be understood in preparation for the coming Sophia revelation. There is a real and present need for the working of Sophia within the different peoples and nations, within the different communities around the world, where there is increasing war and strife.

Mary Sophia lived for a further eleven years on the Earth following the Whitsun event. She remained a few years in the Holy Land and then went with the Apostle John to Ephesus, where she lived not far from the ancient mystery center of Artemis, the temple of Artemis in Ephesus. Through her extraordinary power of clairvoyance, Anne Catherine Emmerich was able to accurately describe the place where the Virgin Mary lived up to the time she departed from the Earth. After reading this description, some priests went to Ephesus and were able to locate the house where Mary had lived. They carried out excavations and found a building, dating back to the first century, corresponding exactly to the plan of the house Anne Catherine Emmerich had described.[5] On the basis of this description the house was reconstructed as a chapel, which is visited by thousands of people each year. It was here that Mary spent the last years of her life, up to the year AD 44, eleven years after the Whitsun event. In that year each of the apostles received an inner call; they came to Ephesus to be present at the death of the Blessed Virgin on the afternoon of August 15, and witnessed her Assumption into heaven that evening.

The Assumption of the Virgin Mary is an event comparable with the Resurrection of Christ Jesus. However, whereas the Resurrection reveals the ultimate goal of Earth evolution in the far distant future, the Ascension of the Virgin Mary reveals a stage prior to this, namely the goal to be attained at the end of our present Earth evolution: the attainment of the Holy City, the Heavenly Jerusalem. Through her Assumption, the Blessed Virgin is already in that condition toward which the whole of humanity is striving. She is the High Priestess of

5. See Bernard F. Deutsch, *Our Lady of Ephesus* (Milwaukee: The Bruce Publishing Company, 1965). The house of Mary was found in 1891.

the Heavenly City. By focusing upon Mary Sophia, we focus upon the goal of our Earth evolution. In the new millennium, during which the Age of Aquarius will begin, an awareness of these Sophianic mysteries connected with Mary Sophia will gradually arise. These mysteries have remained veiled over the course of the preceding 2,000 years of Christianity. But beginning in the twentieth century and continuing throughout the next millennium, they will become more and more central, for these are the mysteries Christ reveals through his Second Coming.

At his coming on the physical plane 2,000 years ago, Christ's great gift was the Lord's Prayer, the 'Our Father'. With the Second Coming, his gift to humanity is the 'Our Mother', the prayer directed to the Mother, the prayer that Valentin Tomberg was able to give around the time of World War II.[6] The 'Our Mother' is central to the New Age of Christianity in which the mysteries of nature are gradually unveiled, bringing an awakening to the etheric realm. In this connection we can think of eurythmy, an art of movement that is concerned with the laws of the etheric body. In eurythmy, although the physical body moves, it does so according to the laws of the etheric body, so that we have in eurythmy a wonderful means of entering into a connection with the etheric realm. It can be a great help in the struggle going on at the present time. For Satan is working to limit our consciousness to the physical plane, so that we do not awaken to the etheric. Everything flooding across our culture that is of a mechanical nature works to draw our consciousness out of the etheric and bind it to the physical plane. Anything, such as eurythmy, that can help elevate our consciousness to the etheric plane, is a help in the present struggle.

We looked earlier at the unfolding of the Christ Impulse according to the rhythm in which one day in the life of Christ corresponds to 29½ years historically. According to this, the period from 1988 up to the year 2018 corresponds to the 39th day of the temptation of

6. Valentin Tomberg spoke of the 'Our Mother' for the first time at Christmas, 1940; see *Starlight*, vol. 5, no. 1 (Spring 2005) for Tomberg's words concerning this prayer (*Starlight* is the newsletter of the Sophia Foundation of North America). This article from *Starlight* is reproduced in the Appendix.

humanity. And the period between 2018 and the year 2047 corresponds to the 40th day. As described in the Gospels, on the 40th day "Angels came and ministered unto him." This belongs to the present century, to the start of the new millennium. It signifies the beginning of a new relationship with the kingdom of the Angels. For those able to pass through the coming trial of materialism, a new relationship to the Angelic beings will open up.

Here, also, eurythmy is of importance. For the movements we make in eurythmy reflect the language of the Angels, and in learning eurythmy we begin to speak their language. One eurythmist described to me that during a near-death experience, as she passed out of her body, she experienced Angelic beings making gestures similar to those made in eurythmy. Thus, eurythmy can be a great help in awakening new faculties belonging to the coming times. Of course there are many other things we have to learn, especially that the work of the Angels with respect to humanity is that of raising human consciousness to a new level of morality.

The development of science up to the present has been concerned primarily with understanding the physical realm and grasping the laws of nature from a physical point of view. However the real task of humanity for the future is to develop a moral world order over and above the natural world order. This is the task for the future. The task of humanity is the development of a moral world order, and the seed of this moral world order is the life of Christ, only part of which is reported in the Gospels. The language Christ Jesus spoke was not the language of philosophy or science. His words are of a purely moral nature. Following the example of Christ, the raising-up of consciousness to develop a moral world order is what will count more and more in the future. The work of the Angels helps us to attain this level. In the religious tradition of the Western Church, Mary Sophia is referred to as the Queen of the Angels, the heart of the Angelic realm. This title is appropriate insofar as she is able to work down on the Archangelic level as the being to whom the Angels look up. The awakening—roughly from the year 2000 onward—to the kingdom of the Angels, signifies at the same time an awakening to Mary Sophia, who embodies a pure moral consciousness.

Returning to the rhythm of the unfolding of the Christ Impulse

into the future, we find something very interesting. At the wedding
at Cana, Christ Jesus performed a great miracle. It took place on the
morning of Wednesday, December 28, in the year AD 29. This was 96
days after the Baptism in the Jordan. If we read the Gospel account
of this miracle, we find the words usually translated in a particular
way. I am referring to when Mary drew attention to Jesus that there
was no wine and that he was responsible for providing the wine. His
reply is usually translated, "What does this mean to thee, woman?"
As Rudolf Steiner pointed out, the true translation of this should
be, "What is it that weaves between thou and me?" In these words
there is an indication that this miracle was the result of a weaving
together between Christ Jesus and Mary Sophia.

Let us look at the wedding at Cana in connection with the rhythm
of one day to 29½ years. Since the wedding took place 96 days after
the Baptism, and since 96 x 29½ = 2828, adding this on to the year
AD 33, we find that in the history of humanity this miracle relates to
the time around the year 2861. Thus it points to the time toward the
end of the millennium that has recently begun. Just as at the beginning of the new millennium there was an opening-up to the kingdom of the Angels, so toward its end there will be a miraculous
event connected with Mary Sophia. This, I believe, has to do with
the new revelation of Sophia, and will occur approximately 500
years after the start of the Age of Aquarius in the year 2375. That is,
500 years after the start of the Age of Aquarius, a miraculous event
will take place that will be relevant to the whole of humanity and
which will be a metamorphosis of the Changing of Water into Wine
at the Wedding at Cana.

All of this is leading toward the goal of human evolution, the
building of the Heavenly City, the New Jerusalem. It entails con-
fronting trials and overcoming them. Whatever form the three
kinds of trials may take, their archetypes are to be found in the three
temptations in the wilderness. And since we are at present living in
the historical period of the temptation of humanity, it may be helpful to look at the nature of these three temptations and how they
may be overcome.

The *first temptation* is described as falling down to worship
Lucifer, who reveals all the glory of this world. This is the temptation

of the will to power, which worked in an unprecedented way in the arising of the Führer in Germany in 1933—exactly the time when the new revelation of Christ in the etheric was beginning. This was a counter-impulse to the new Christ revelation. It presented itself in the form of a temptation to worship an individual who promised everything. All he demanded was obedience and devotion to himself. Christ answered this temptation with the words, "You shall worship the Lord your God and him only shall you serve." This means that the human being should never give up his or her own self ('I') to any being other than God. This temptation to worship a human being for some reason exists in countless forms all around us. It is nothing other than a modern form of paganism. We can have reverence and devotion for someone's teaching, but it is nothing other than idolatry to worship that person. This temptation of the will to power is found everywhere in the modern world.

The working of this temptation is well known in the Christian tradition, and a certain spiritual practice is cultivated to overcome it: the vow of *obedience*. Obedience is practiced in the monastic orders as one of the three vows. It is the antidote to the will to power and is based on the practice of aligning one's will with Divine Will ("Not my will, but thy will be done"). As a source for the power of obedience we can turn to the first of the seven stages of the Passion: the *washing of the feet*, which entails humility.

The *second temptation* is that of plunging from the pinnacle of the temple. The tempter said to Christ that if he made this plunge, "the Angels will bear you up." This is the temptation to plunge from the domain of 'I'-consciousness into the realm of the subconscious, trusting that one will be borne up by one's subconscious impulses. The plunge from the pinnacle of the temple amounts to casting oneself down from the clear light of 'I'-consciousness that is characterized by our faculties of conscience and rational thought. The temptation to desert the pinnacle of the temple is ubiquitous in the present-day world, facilitated by alcohol or drugs, or any kind of intoxication that leads from clear ego consciousness into the domain of subconscious forces.

In the monastic orders the antidote to this temptation is the vow of *chastity*. This may be understood as a chastity of consciousness in which solely the voice of conscience is heeded, and only what is clearly transparent on the level of logical thought is accepted. This practice helps overcome the temptation of plunging from the pinnacle of the temple. A source for the practice of chastity is found in the second stage of the Passion, the *scourging*. Everyone who opens up a connection with the spiritual world immediately experiences from different sides a scourging aimed at breaking that connection. The capacity to stand firm and be driven neither to the right nor to the left is the power of chastity understood in a spiritual sense.

The *third temptation*, that of *turning stones into bread*, is the temptation of materialism. It is the temptation of laying claim to anything material and making it one's spiritual possession. This temptation is combated in the monastic tradition through the vow of *poverty*, which entails renunciation and not accepting anything on a material level as one's own. An inner source for the practice of poverty is found in the third stage of the Passion: the *crowning with thorns*. Here Christ was able to stand in perfect humility, conscious solely of the spiritual world as superior to the physical one. The whole temptation of materialism is based on placing the material above the spiritual. A person crowned with thorns is someone awake to the kingdom of the spirit, awake to conscience, crowned by the world of the spirit. This new kingdom is attained at the expense of renouncing possession of the material.

The three traditional vows of obedience, chastity, and poverty are a bulwark for overcoming the three temptations. These vows may be understood on a spiritual level, and such an understanding of them has been given in the twentieth century in the work *Meditations on the Tarot*, which contains profound insight into the workings of the temptations. The three vows of obedience, chastity, and poverty have been largely forgotten in our culture, which signifies that Christ also has been largely forgotten, for it is through the three vows that one unites with the being of Christ. These three vows practiced by the monks and nuns of the monastic orders relate to the consequences of the Fall as a path of atonement for sin.

However, it is not sufficient simply to atone. The consequences of the Fall must be combatted actively and overcome. And for this there are the three vows taken by the knights of the Middle Ages: the

vows of *courage, faithfulness,* and *righteousness.* The three vows of
the monastic orders (obedience, chastity, and poverty) represent the
feminine side, relating to atonement, and bring us into connection
with the Son, Christ; the three knightly vows of courage, faithfulness, and righteousness represent the *masculine* side, signifying an
activation of the will, and bring us into connection with the Father.

If the knightly vows are practiced by themselves without the
monastic vows, they may bring catastrophe, because they signify an
intensification of self-will. This is the main problem in the world
today. There is too much self-will. The stronger self-will becomes,
the more Christ is forgotten. Thus the knightly vows need to be
practiced together with the monastic vows. For example, obedience
needs to be practiced together with courage. In practicing obedience by itself, there is a danger of becoming passive. But if one com-
bines practicing obedience while also practicing courage, one
remains active and is able to go forward. Similarly, the practice of
chastity belongs together with the practice of faithfulness, to balance out the possibility that through chastity alone, one could lose
one's inner sense of purpose and direction. Faithfulness to higher
ideals ensures purpose and direction. Actually, faithfulness requires
more courage and endurance than simply practicing courage itself.
Whereas the force of courage may be drawn from the fourth stage of
the Passion, the carrying of the cross, the quality of faithfulness may
be drawn from the fifth stage of the Passion, the *crucifixion.* This is
faithfulness to the higher self, which is able to pass through the crucifixion. Lastly, the practice of the vow of poverty is complemented
through the practice of righteousness. The strength of righteousness may be drawn from the sixth stage of the Passion, the *laying in
the grave,* which signifies making the concerns of all the Earth one's
own, then uniting oneself with the whole Earth by laying oneself in
the grave. The practice of righteousness entails extending one's concerns beyond one's immediate personal sphere, and this helps balance out the possibility of a lack of concern that could arise through
a one-sided practice of poverty.

The forces needed in the future to overcome the different temptations are to be found in the Christian tradition—on the one hand
in the three vows of the monastic tradition, and on the other in the

three vows of the knightly tradition. These are related to the first six stages of the Passion. With the seventh stage, the stage of *resurrection*, the sun-filled force of the knights and the monks combined, the masculine and the feminine, works to raise everything up to a higher level. The unfolding of Christianity has already provided much that is needed for the future. With the new impulse of Christianity coming in our time, opening up the Sophianic mysteries, a way may be found into the new millennium. This is bound up with the heavenly sign of the Son of Man.

The Sign of the
Son of Man in Heaven

IN THE GOSPEL OF ST MATTHEW the disciples ask Christ "What will be the sign of your coming and of the close of the age?" This question concerns his Second Coming, and Christ's answer is lengthy. In the course of answering he uses the word tribulation three times. He says to the disciples, "They will deliver you up to tribulation and put you to death. You will be hated by all nations for my name's sake." Later he says, "Then there will be great tribulation such as has not been from the beginning of the world until now, no, and never will be." And further, "Immediately after the tribulation of those days, the Sun will be darkened and the Moon will not give its light, and the stars will fall from heaven, and the powers of the heavens will be shaken. Then shall appear the sign of the Son of Man in heaven." These words give a response to the question, "What will be the sign of your coming? When will you come again?" A period of tribulation is indicated, then the end of this period of tribulation, followed by the appearance of the sign of the Son of Man in heaven. This gives some background to the question of the Second Coming of Christ.

As referred to already, through the Second Coming of Christ a new revelation connected with the mysteries of Sophia—with the Sophianic Trinity of Mother, Daughter, and Holy Soul—is taking place. It is actually through the Second Coming of Christ that these mysteries, which were more or less closed off 2,000 years ago, are now being opened up again. To understand the background to this, we must take account of the polarity of the Father in heaven, the *transcendental* being of Divine Love, and the Mother, who is the *immanent* being of creation, the spiritual origin of all matter— the word 'mother' being related to the word 'matter'. This is a fundamental existential polarity, one that has been essentially veiled during the last 2,000 years of Christianity.

In Rudolf Steiner's life-work we find mention of the Mother. In fact, he gives a wonderful meditation that can help us relate to the Mother. In this meditation he describes the Mother as spread out through the whole of creation. She speaks to humanity:

> *If you seek me with true desire for knowledge,*
> *I shall be with you.*
> *I am the seed and the source of the physical world.*
> *I am the ocean of light in which your soul lives.*
> *I am the ruler of space,*
> *I am the creator of cycles of time.*
> *Fire, air, light, water and earth obey me.*
> *Feel me as the spiritual origin of all matter.*
> *And as I have no consort on Earth, call me Maya.*[1]

These words give us a feeling for the Mother as Mistress of the Elements. This was a common expression in the ancient mysteries connected with the Mother. She rules the elements, and orders the cycles of time. She is the ruler of space, and human souls live in her ocean of light. She is the seed and the source of all creation. In the closing words to this meditation, the Mother speaks the words: *And as I have no consort on Earth, call me Maya.* Here the Hindu conception of the world as Maya, as illusion, comes to expression. It is a matter of awakening to the realization that we are living within this divine being, that every minute of our lives we are supported by her, that we could not live for a moment without her life-giving forces. For as long as we do not realize this, we are living in Maya. This means that we do not see the world as it really is. However, there are stages of awakening to the Mother, and these are coming about now through the Second Coming of Christ, through his renewed activity in the etheric world.

One aspect of this is an awakening to the world of the elements, which comprises the nature spirits. This awakening is also connected

1. See Appendix: *The Divine Mother.*

with finding the lost kingdom of the Mother, known in the East as Shamballa. A new experience of Shamballa is coming, enabled especially by directing our attention toward the center of the Earth—toward the heart of the Mother—and to the flow of life forces that stream thence into all living beings. This is one stage of awakening to the Mother—signifying raising the veil of Maya. At this stage there is an awakening to the four elements of fire, air, water, and earth.

A further stage is awakening to the realm of the planets. How are we related to the seven planets? How is our inner being built up out of the planetary realms? Every human being has a special connection with one or another planet, or perhaps with several planets. At the end of his life, Rudolf Steiner began to open up something of these mysteries. For example, he indicated that Goethe was especially connected with the sphere of Jupiter, and Schiller with the sphere of Saturn; and he gave other examples as well. Becoming conscious of the realm of the planets also belongs to the awakening to the Mother.

A still higher stage of awakening to the Mother entails becoming aware of our connection with the twelve signs of the zodiac. Awakening to the Mother is at the same time a journey through the four elements and through the seven planets to the twelve signs of the zodiac. The mysteries of the twelve signs of the zodiac are connected with the human 'I', the self. Just as there are fundamentally seven soul types connected with the seven planets, and just as there are four temperaments connected with the four elements, so there are twelve spiritual orientations according to the human being's connection with the zodiacal realm of the fixed stars. Something of this mystery is indicated by the fact that Christ Jesus had twelve apostles, mirroring the twelve signs of the zodiac. In our working together we have been trying to come to an understanding of this highest aspect of the created realm of the cosmos, striving toward an awakening to the twelve signs of the zodiac. And through eurythmy we have the possibility of entering into an inner relationship with these cosmic realms.

We have been considering the polarity of the Father and Mother as the primal polarity of creation. There is also the polarity Son : Daughter; that is, Son-Logos-Christ : Daughter-Divine Wisdom-Sophia. We can begin to awaken more and more intensely to this fundamental polarity. Every thought of Christ can lead us also to Sophia. Similarly, the more intensely we relate to Sophia, the more we are led to Christ. Rudolf Steiner spoke of this as one of the holy mysteries of our time: through experiencing Christ within us, we shall find Sophia; and through awakening to Sophia, we find Christ. How can we better understand this view of evolution?

This morning we were working with eurythmy as a metamorphosis of the sacred temple dance of the Egyptian mysteries. Central to these mysteries was devotion to Isis and Osiris. The main intent of the Egyptian mysteries was to awaken a living experience of Isis and Osiris. These two beings, Isis and Osiris, were always seen together, working together, weaving together. The Egyptians looked up to them as the pre-Christian cosmic manifestations of the beings we call Sophia and Christ. For the Egyptians to speak of Osiris and Isis was equivalent to our saying Christ and Sophia. In the Hermes mysteries of ancient Egypt, there was a pre-vision of the incarnation of Christ. Christ was seen as Horus, the Divine Son, born of Isis, whereby Horus, although the son of Osiris, was seen as identical to Osiris, appearing in a younger form. Christ, seen by the Egyptians as Osiris—and in younger form as Horus—incarnated in human form in Jesus at the Baptism in the Jordan. Isis took on human form in Mary, becoming Mary Sophia at Pentecost. The incarnation of these two divine beings took place at the turning point of time for the redemption of the Earth and humanity. In this age of the Second Coming, where there is a renewed working of Christ within the aura of the Earth, there is at the same time a renewed working of Sophia. These two beings lead us into the future, toward the future goal of evolution, toward the arising of the Heavenly City, the holy city of Heavenly Jerusalem. In the Apocalypse, the Book of Revelation, we are given a wonderful imaginative depiction of the Heavenly City. There our attention is drawn to the Lamb, Jesus Christ, and to his Bride, who is Sophia. We also find in the Book of Revelation a sublime imagination of Sophia as the Woman Clothed with the Sun, with the Moon under her feet, and on her head a crown of twelve stars. Here she manifests herself as the soul of the cosmos.

The significance of the Assumption of the Blessed Virgin Mary eleven years after the Mystery of Golgotha was, as has been pointed out, that she became the first human being to enter into the condition that human beings will attain in the future paradise. This is the new paradise that replaces what was lost through the Fall, the new paradise being the Heavenly Jerusalem. The Blessed Virgin Mary was the first human being to enter this new paradise. It is she who beckons to humanity from the center of this future condition toward which the whole of evolution is leading. Thus, in speaking of Christ and Sophia, we may think of these wonderful images of the Lamb and his Bride in the Book of Revelation. The sacred wedding feast of the Bride and the Lamb is described there also.

Let us look now at the third polarity, that of the Holy Spirit and Holy Soul. The Holy Spirit weaves between the transcendental Father in heaven and the Son incarnated on the Earth. It is the Holy Spirit who brings enlightenment to humanity, who is the spiritualizer of our existence, who makes us conscious. Just as we can conceive of the weaving of the Holy Spirit between the transcendental Father and the incarnated Son, so the Holy Soul weaves between the Divine Sophia, the soul of the cosmos, and the Mother, who is the Mother of everything living. And just as the Holy Spirit works to spiritualize the whole of creation, so the Holy Soul works to sanctify, to make holy, everything in existence. Whenever we feel moments of holiness touching our lives, this is a manifestation of the working of the Holy Soul. Something of the weaving of the Holy Soul is present whenever human beings come together in harmony and work together in the same spirit. The Holy Soul then weaves between the souls of those who come together in community.

In our civilization, forces actively work against all the new spiritual impulses trying to come through. For example, there are forces at work to desecrate everything that is holy and sacred; forces at work to disrupt community life and all working together of human beings united in a common spiritual impulse; and forces at work to mechanize everything that is living—as referred to earlier, the goal of Satan is to take hold of the elemental kingdom, the etheric ocean around the Earth, for his own blood, and also to take possession of human blood. Thus, the impulse of Christ at work in the etheric is vital for the survival of the Earth. And a new Christian wisdom of the stars related to the life of Christ, with this life at its center, will help to give us an orientation and a deeper understanding of the times in which we are living. As discussed earlier, the period between the Baptism in the Jordan and the Mystery of Golgotha was a kind of embryonic period, where a seed was laid in the Earth for the creation of a new cosmos. Since the Mystery of Golgotha, this embryonic seed impulse has been unfolding through history according to the rhythm of one day in the life of Christ corresponding to 29½ years. This is the Saturn rhythm. Why the Saturn rhythm? The planet Saturn is the bearer of cosmic memory. Saturn moves through the zodiac once in 29½ years. All that happens is remembered in the sphere of Saturn. And as the most important impulse for the history of Earth was the life of Christ, culminating in the 3½ years of his ministry, every day of this is remembered in the Saturn sphere. Every day of these 3½ years unfolds with the orbit—with the 29½-year rhythm—of Saturn around the zodiac.

According to this, the period between 1988 and the year 2018—the time of Saturn's orbit around the zodiac from sidereal Sagittarius back to Sagittarius—is the 39th day of the period of the 40 days of temptation. This period of the temptation of all humanity began in the year AD 869, at which time Saturn was in sidereal Sagittarius. This was the historical year representing to first 'day' of the temptation of humanity. We are now approaching the end of this period. The end of the 40th day will be reached by the middle of the century. Looking at the life of Christ, these 40 days were clearly a very difficult time, a time of trial and temptation, which culminated in the three temptations on the last three days. Correspondingly, the present point in history is a very difficult time for the whole of humanity, a time when we are confronted with very strong temptations. However, just as the temptations of Christ were necessary, insofar as he had to overcome them to enable the unfolding of his mission, so the temptations coming now are necessary for the unfolding of the mission of humanity. The three temptations are nothing other than the consequences of the three aspects of the Fall spoken of earlier; and the Christ Impulse is the healing impulse for the overcoming of the consequences of the Fall. The three temptations signify the working on through history of the consequences of the Fall: the temptation of the will to power—the *first* temptation;

the temptation of casting oneself down from the pinnacle of the temple—the *second* temptation; and the changing of stones into bread—the *third* temptation. Each of these is related to one of the three aspects of the Fall, the consequences of which were toil, suffering, and death. As referred to earlier, the conscious spiritual path of meditation, of purification through overcoming suffering by taking it voluntarily upon oneself, and of initiation as the voluntary passing through death, comprise the way of overcoming the three primal curses, which were the consequences of the Fall.

The vows of obedience, chastity and poverty are practices which, understood in the spiritual sense, contain the forces for the overcoming of the temptations. Let us consider this in relation to the third temptation, turning stones into bread, which is connected with the primal curse of death. To fall prey to the third temptation means to fall into the material realm, the kingdom of death. Materialism is the way this third temptation presents itself to humanity. This is the satanic temptation that is now waxing stronger and stronger, for the third temptation is the special temptation belonging to the 39th day of the 40 days of temptation in which humanity now finds itself. Historically, it was on the 39th day in the wilderness that the encounter between Christ and Satan, took place. This was marked by a special cosmic configuration, a conjunction of the Sun and Pluto in 9 degrees sidereal Sagittarius. Historically this was on November 29th in the year AD 29. This was the 39th day of the period in the wilderness. In this meeting between the Sun and Pluto we see the cosmic sign of the third temptation, the encounter between Christ and Satan (or Ahriman). This whole period of the temptation, the forty days in the wilderness, began historically, in the time of Christ, when the Sun entered Scorpio. Since the Sun travels one degree in the zodiac each day, the first thirty days of temptation coincided with the Sun moving through the 30 degrees of the sidereal sign of Scorpio, and the last ten days corresponded to the Sun moving through the first 10 degrees of the sidereal sign of Sagittarius. With the conjunction of the Sun and Pluto at 9 degrees Sagittarius, the culmination of the whole of the period of temptation was reached. We are now living in the corresponding time for humanity as a whole—the period between 1988 and 2018. The remarkable thing is that in the year 2010 Pluto will be at 9 degrees Sagittarius, exactly where it was at the time of this conjunction on the 39th day in the wilderness. Thus we can expect the encounter with the third temptation of materialism to reach a certain climax around 2010.

This is a time of tribulation, as expressed in Christ's words. In the Gospel of Matthew he characterizes the period of tribulation as a time of wars, famines, and earthquakes. And this is precisely the hallmark of our time. We need only think of the two World Wars (and all the other wars), and also of the famines around the world; and the third sign—earthquakes—is certainly characteristic of the past century as well. In fact, there is the ever-present possibility of destruction through earthquake in our time.[2]

But let us return to the question of the sign of the Son of Man in heaven. As we have said, Christ manifested himself in a different form in each of the astrological ages connected with the precession of the equinoxes, each lasting 2,160 years. The Age of Cancer in ancient India saw Christ as *Vishvakarma* in connection with the realm of the fixed stars. The Age of Gemini in ancient Persian saw Christ as *Ahura Mazdao*, the aura of the Sun. The Egyptians referred to Christ as *Osiris*, who came down from the Sun, united himself with the Moon, and was worshipped by them in connection with the waxing and waning of the Moon. In the Age of Aries, Christ took on flesh and was named the *Lamb of God*. In the Age of Pisces the symbolism for Christ is connected with the *Fish*. The symbol for *Christ* among the early Christians was simply the vertical line, connecting Heaven and Earth, and the symbol for *Jesus* was the cross.) = *Christ*; ✕ = *Jesus*; ✶ = *Jesus Christ*. This sign was seen as the symbol of Jesus Christ. This is also the hieroglyph for fish (✶ = fish). The Greek word for fish is ΙΧΘΥΣ —*Ichthys* (*I-Ch-Th-Y-S*), which was interpreted as *I*eßoūs *Ch*ristòs *Th*eoū (h) *Y*iòs *S*otér,

---

2. The underwater earthquake off the coast of Sumatra on December 26, 2004 caused a *tsunami* through which more than 283,000 people lost their lives, and the Kashmir earthquake on October 8, 2005 claimed the lives of more than 87,000 people—just to mention two recent examples.

meaning Jesus Christ, God's Son, Saviour. Among the early Christians he was referred to as Jesus Ichthys or Jesus the Fish.

Son of Man is a new designation for Christ in the Gospels. The Age of Pisces will end in the year 2375, when the vernal point will pass from Pisces to Aquarius. This is the "closing of the age." As described in the Gospel of Matthew, the disciples asked, "What will be the signs of the close of the age?" And in answer Christ speaks of the appearance of the sign of the Son of Man in heaven. He is referring to the beginning of the Age of Aquarius. The sign of the Son of Man in heaven points to the working of Christ as the Aquarian Waterman. The Waterman can be regarded as a cosmic symbol of the etheric body in the human being. The etheric organism is that which lives in the watery element within us. Thus the Waterman in the human being is the etheric body. The sign of the Son of Man in heaven is, then, the Waterman; it has to do with the entrance of the vernal point into Aquarius, the time when the guiding forces of civilization will work from the sidereal sign of Aquarius just as they now work from Pisces.

As we have seen, the year 1899 is the beginning of the New Age, signifying the start of a new working-in of Christ in his etheric body. We are living now in the period between 1899 and the start of the Aquarian Age, and we must clearly distinguish between the two.

Let us recall what the New Age is. The year 1899 signified the end of the 5,000-year period known as Kali Yuga, which started in the year 3102 BC. During the Kali Yuga, the Dark Age, human consciousness was increasingly cut off from the spiritual world. According to Hindu chronology, Kali Yuga, also known as the Iron Age, was the fourth Yuga, each Yuga or age being characterized by a metal: gold, silver, bronze, and iron. If one follows the Hindu chronology, Kali Yuga lasted 5,000 years and the preceding Yuga lasted 10,000 years. We see that time is accelerating. And this continues, for the following Yuga, the New Age that began in 1899, lasts only 2,500 years. In other words, the present Yuga, which started in 1899, will last until about the year 4400. It is important to recall here that the accelerating rhythm of the four Yugas is a different rhythm than that of the regular 2,160-year rhythm of the zodiacal ages. Turning, then, to the zodiacal Age of Aquarius, we see that its 2,160-year duration will overspan the period 2375–4535. Therefore, the (zodiacal) Age of Aquarius will last slightly longer (136 years) than the (yugic) New Age, which in Hindu terminology is called *Satya Yuga*, which can be translated as Age of Light. The close of Satya Yuga coincides more or less (to within 140 years) with the end of the Aquarian Age. To summarize—New Age: 1899–4399; Aquarian Age: 2375–4535: present period leading up to the start of the Aquarian Age: 1899–2375. Thus, roughly speaking, the New Age comprises the present period from 1899 up to the start of the Aquarian Age—plus the Aquarian Age. And it is precisely the present period that is referred to in the Gospel of Matthew as the period of tribulation preceding the appearance of the sign of the Son of Man in heaven.

What does this mean? At the start of the Age of Aquarius, when new cosmic forces will begin to work here on the Earth, there will be a general awakening to the etheric realm. The etheric forces will be stimulated during the Age of Aquarius. This is symbolized by the Waterman, associated with the etheric body of the human being, connected in turn with the etheric realm of nature. We are approaching this time of awakening to the etheric, and this entails an awakening to the Mother and her kingdom, which is designated in the East as Shamballa, and has to do with the elemental realms. In the time preceding this—the present period of tribulation—the possibility exists through the renewed working of Christ's etheric body in this New Age of connecting to the event of the Second Coming, of awakening even now to the etheric world. On the other hand, the power of materialism grows progressively stronger, working to cut humanity off from the etheric world and to blot out any experience of the Second Coming of Christ. This is the real struggle of the present time. It is a struggle between falling prey to materialism, which fetters consciousness to the physical, and an awakening through Christ and Sophia to the etheric. All the trials and tribulations of our day are connected with this conflict. The Gospel of Matthew speaks of the signs of this period of tribulation as wars, famines, and earthquakes. (In this context, 'earthquakes' may be taken to signify natural catastrophes in general.)

A positive development we can point to in this regard is the awakening, in the ecology movement, to the realization that everything within the human being, everything that he or she does, has its effect upon nature. This means that the human being's soul life works in such a way that, if it is not harmonious, natural catastrophes will result. The reality behind these predictions of earthquakes, or natural disasters, is, then, that they can be evoked by humanity's misdeeds.

However, when people seek to awaken to a new consciousness of nature and strive to bring their own soul life into inner harmony, the possibility exists to counteract the influences of chaos arising in the world around us. This possibility is given and strengthened by Christ, who is working for those striving to become spiritually conscious in this age of tribulation. As is written in the Gospel of Matthew: "When the sign of the Son of Man appears in heaven, all the tribes of the Earth will mourn, and they will behold him," and in the first chapter of the Book of Revelation: "Behold, he is coming with the clouds, and every eye will see him, and all peoples of the Earth will lament on account of him." This indicates the general awakening to the Second Coming of Christ in the Age of Aquarius. Yet there is also the possibility of awakening to this now, and through this to awaken to the Mother,[3] to the Divine Sophia, and to the Holy Soul. Hopefully this outline of a new Christian wisdom of the stars will help to give some understanding of the task for the future, the task of a healthy evolution for the Earth, and the task of humanity to find its right path. And as referred to at the beginning, the opportunity presented to those living on the West Coast is a very special one, since the West Coast is the point of influx of these new etheric forces connected with Christ, working in along the West Coast and flowing from here across the rest of the world.

---

3. See Appendix: *The Divine Mother.*

Appendix:
The Divine Mother

In the Sophia Foundation newsletter, *Starlight*, articles of interest translated from Valentin Tomberg's literary estate are gradually appearing. These are esoteric articles that have never been published before, including the following one on the Divine Mother. At the core of the Sophia Foundation is the spiritual work with the Lord's Prayer Course, also designated—in its later continuation—as the 'Our Mother' Course. This course is the spiritual legacy of a great spiritual teacher, Valentin Tomberg, whose name in his twentieth-century incarnation (1900–1973) is largely unknown, even though it is a matter of one of the great spiritual teachers of humanity.

Through him have come spiritual treasures such as the Prayer Sequence that many friends of the Sophia Foundation are working with. Central to the Prayer Sequence is the new prayer for humanity in the present age of Christ's Second Coming: the 'Our Mother' Prayer, which is complementary to the 'Our Father' (Lord's Prayer) taught by Jesus Christ two thousand years ago. The 'Our Mother' Prayer was given through Valentin Tomberg in the Russian language at a special moment in time, as revealed in the following article. In this article from Christmas 1940, the 'Our Mother' Prayer is not referred to explicitly, but various petitions (of the seven petitions of this prayer) clearly shine through the words. A short time later, some of Valentin Tomberg's students began working with the 'Our Mother' Prayer in the context of the Lord's Prayer Course that he gave in Amsterdam during World War II. The following article is of particular interest as it is evidently the first time that Valentin Tomberg said anything at all about the meaning of what is expressed in the 'Our Mother' Prayer, given to him at this moment when the world was under such dark clouds of war.

The word 'article' was used above, but to be more precise Valentin Tomberg spoke these words within the context of a small group of people attending the Lord's Prayer Course in Amsterdam. His words were written down, and so it would be more correct to say 'lecture' than 'article'. But unfortunately, possibly due to a lack of completeness in the transcription of his words, there are several gaps in understanding the text which, where appropriate, I have filled with explanatory words in brackets [ ]. This prayer is the spiritual 'Foundation Stone' of the Sophia Foundation of North America, and so may also be of interest to readers of *The Sign of the Son of Man in Heaven: Sophia and the New Star Wisdom*.

OUR MOTHER

VALENTIN TOMBERG
(CHRISTMAS 1940)

Christmas this year was, spiritually, Easter, since the World Soul resurrected as memory. Until this time humanity still lived according to the Ten Commandments, which however have an infinitely greater content [than is commonly known] and which need to be understood ever more deeply. For example, by "Thou shalt not take my name in vain" is to be further understood that one ought not acknowledge anyone else in life as 'Führer' [leader].

"Thou shalt not make any graven image" appeals to moral intuition, so that one goes [one's way] freely and inwardly, connecting oneself imagelessly with one's God.

"Honor your Father and Mother" refers not simply to our physical parents, but also to our Father in heaven and our Earth Mother. The Earth Mother is not to be found; [She] has been extinguished from consciousness completely [in modern Western civilization at that time].

Where can we find Her?

One comes to the Father through the seven stages of death [which correspond to the soul's passage in the life after death through the seven planetary spheres: Moon, Mercury, Venus, Sun, Mars, Jupiter, Saturn]. In each sphere through which one ascends to the Father, a part [of oneself] is left behind, something is peeled off. Finally [after completing the passage through the seven planetary spheres] one ascends as a purely spiritual being into the realm of the Father, where [generally] one loses consciousness.

The way to the Earth Mother leads through the sub-earthly spheres.[1] There one finds Her and eternal life. After encountering the Mother one can resurrect. Christ, the Son, reconnected the Father and the Mother, who are separated by substance and by evil, the belt of lies. Human beings also have the task of once again bringing about this connection.

Through Christ's descent into hell, whereby He encountered the Mother, thus making the Resurrection and Ascension possible, there arose [Sacred] Magic through the connection of above and below. One cannot rule substance, [but] can only master it from within.

The Mother has hidden Herself; [She] has fled into the interior of the Earth. And so She was actually forgotten for a time. But now at this Christmas time [there] has resurrected the first [thing] which indicates a gradual understanding and seeking of the Earth Mother again: *the remembrance of Her name.*

The human soul has no place on Earth [nor] also in the spiritual world—for there [is] the spirit, not the soul. Paradise was the realm of the soul; it has disappeared into the interior of the Earth with the Mother. Paradise, Shamballa, is our home; without it we are homeless wanderers.

However, Christ—after His death—encountered the Tree of Life. One may thus hope that Shamballa will appear again on Earth. Shamballa is not something spatial. [It] is not a place, but a state of consciousness that is present always and everywhere. It is the Earth's etheric body permeated with the breath of Buddhi.

---

1. See Robert Powell, *The Christ Mystery* (Fair Oaks, CA: Rudolf Steiner College Press, 1999), chap. 3, 'Sub-Nature and the Second Coming'.

And in the coming kingdom one will experience how the Mother warms homeless souls, and then how one can be truly faithful from within, naturally. At present we are, naturally, still unfaithful, [but] then [in the future], there will be in human hearts, as a stream of daily bread, a daily memory/thought of the name of the Mother.

In the future, forgetting the name of the Mother will be experienced as a sin of omission ['Schuld']. And one will take up the fight against evil in the world, against the temptation that brought about [not only] the disappearance of Paradise [but also that] the Mother remained in the darkness. The immeasurable pain of the Father— through the separation from the Mother—will be stilled through the Son. To Sophia belongs the homeland and the bestowal [of wisdom] and the all-merciful grace for everything in the All.

The essence of the above words spoken by Valentin Tomberg at Christmas 1940 is to be found in the 'Our Mother' Prayer:

Our Mother, Thou who art in the darkness of the underworld,
May the holiness of Thy name shine anew in our remembering,
May the breath of Thy awakening kingdom
   warm the hearts of all who wander homeless.
May the resurrection of Thy will renew eternal faith
   even unto the depths of physical substance.
Receive this day the living memory of Thee from human hearts,
Who implore Thee to forgive the sin of forgetting Thee,
And are ready to fight against temptation,
Which has led Thee to existence in darkness,
That through the Deed of the Son,
The immeasurable pain of the Father be stilled,
By the liberation of all beings from the tragedy of Thy withdrawal.
For Thine is the homeland and the boundless wisdom
   and the all-merciful grace.
For all and everything in the Circle of All.
Amen.

Valentin Tomberg was not the first spiritual teacher of the twentieth century to speak about the Divine Mother. Before him, Rudolf Steiner (1861–1925) had spoken of the Mother, though only on a few occasions, the most well-known being in the context of the 'Uriel Imagination' that can be experienced most strongly around the time of the summer solstice (St. John's Tide):

The silver-sparkling blue below, arising from the depths of the Earth and bound up with human weakness and error, is gathered into a picture of the Earth Mother. Whether She is called Demeter or Mary, the picture is of the Earth Mother. So it is that in directing our gaze downward, we cannot do otherwise than bring together in Imagination all those secrets of the depths that go to make up the material Mother of all existence. While in all that which is concentrated in the flowing from above, we feel and experience the Spirit Father of everything around us. And now we behold the outcome of the working together of the Spirit Father with the Earth Mother, bearing so beautifully within itself the harmony of the earthly silver and the gold of the heights. Between the Father and the Mother we behold the Son.[2]

Rudolf Steiner also gave an inspiring meditation on the Divine Mother:

If you seek me with true desire for knowledge, I shall be with you.
I am the seed and the source of your visible world.
I am the ocean of light in which your soul lives.
I am the ruler of space.
I am the creator of cycles of time.
Fire, Air, Light, Water, and Earth obey me.
Feel Me as the spiritual origin of all matter.
And as I have no consort on earth, call Me Maya.[3]

This meditation belonged to the second grade of Rudolf Steiner's Esoteric School, which he led from 1904 to 1914, and it was accompanied by the words: *One imagines a Feminine Form spread out in the universe.*[4]

2. Ibid, p32.
3. Translated by Robert Powell, *Divine Sophia, Holy Wisdom* (Palo Alto, CA: Sophia Foundation of North America, 2003), p11.
4. Ibid.

Another person who has contributed in the twentieth century to the unveiling of the mystery of the Divine Mother is the great Russian seer and poet Daniel Andreev (1906–1959), who wrote the following words in his masterpiece *The Rose of the World*, which was written (for the most part) in the 1950s when he was in Vladimir prison, where he been sentenced to twenty-five years imprisonment under Stalin. Andreev's words are a passionate plea to honor the Earth Mother, known in the Bible as *the Mother of everything living* (Gen. 3:20).

Earth is the Mother of all the others, and not only of them, but of every living thing: every elemental, every animal, human, dae-mon, angel, demon, and even every angelic hierarchy. An inex-haustible wellspring, She is the one who creates the ether body of all beings and takes part along with the individual monads in the creation of their astral bodies. She is endowed with warm, inex-haustible love for everything, even demons. She grieves for them, but forgives them. Everyone, even angels of darkness, call Her 'Mother'. She loves all and everything, but She reveres only the highest hierarchies, especially Christ. She is fertilized by the great radiant Spirits of the Sun. She perceives people and their inner world. She hears and responds to the call of our heart, and She answers through Love and through Nature. May Her Name be blessed! Prayer can and should be offered up to Her in great humility.

All of us abided at one time in Her immaculate heart. Great One of Light! They sang Your glory in the temples of Egypt and ancient Greece, on the banks of the Ganges and on the top of the ziggurats of Ur, in the Land of the Rising Sun, and in the far West, on the Andean plateaus. We all love You—good and bad, wise and ignorant, believers and nonbelievers, those who feel the infinite goodness of Your heart, and those who simply enjoy Your light and warmth. Cascades of spiritual grace pour down into the angelic worlds, the worlds of the elementals, and the worlds of humanity. Beautiful Spirit, the origin and sire of all liv-ing matter, the visible image and likeness of the Universal Sun, the living icon of the One God, allow me too to join my voice, audible to You alone, to the global chorus of Your praise. Love us, O Radiant One![5]

ABOUT ROBERT POWELL, PH.D.

Robert is an internationally known lecturer, author, eurythmist and movement therapist. He is founder of the Choreocosmos School of Cosmic and Sacred Dance, and co-founder of the Sophia Foundation of North America. He received his doctorate for his thesis on the *History of the Zodiac*, now available as a book from Sophia Academic Press. His other published works include: *The Sophia Teachings*, a six tape series (Sounds True Recordings), as well as the following books: *Divine Sophia-Holy Wisdom, The Most Holy Trinosophia and the New Revelation of the Divine Feminine, The Sophia Teachings, Chronicle of the Living Christ, Christian Hermetic Astrology, The Christ Mystery, The Morning Meditation in Eurythmy,* and the yearly *Christian Star Calendar*. He translated the spiritual classic *Meditations on the Tarot* and co-translated Valentin Tomberg's *Lazarus, Come Forth!* He is co-author with Lacquanna Paul of *Cosmic Dances of the Zodiac* and *Cosmic Dances of the Planets*. He teaches a gentle form of healing movement: the sacred dance of eurythmy (from the Greek, meaning 'harmonious movement') as well as the cosmic dances of the planets and signs of the zodiac, and through the Sophia Grail Circle he facilitates sacred celebrations dedicated to the Divine Feminine. Robert offers workshops in Europe and North America and, with Karen Rivers, co-founder of the Sophia Foundation, leads pilgrimages to the world's sacred sites (1996 Turkey; 1997 Holy Land; 1998 France; 2000 Britain; 2002 Italy; 2004 Greece; 2006 Egypt; 2008 India).—see http://www.sophiafoundation.org.

5. Daniel Andreev, *The Rose of the World* (Gt. Barrington, MA: Lindisfarne Press, 1997), p280.

www.ingramcontent.com/pod-product-compliance
Lightning Source LLC
LaVergne TN
LVHW091158080426
835509LV00006B/742